Circular Fashion

LAURENCE KING

Published by
Laurence King Publishing
361–373 City Road
London EC1V 1LR
United Kingdom
Tel: +44 20 7841 6900
Email: enquiries@laurenceking.com
www.laurenceking.com

A catalog record for this book is available from the British Library.

ISBN: 978-1-78627-887-6

Commissioning Editor: Sophie Wise
Senior Editor: Katherine Pitt
Illustrations: Akio Morishima
Design: Two Sheds
Picture research: Giulia Hetherington

Printed in China

Laurence King Publishing is committed to ethical and sustainable
production. We are proud participants in the Book Chain Project®.

bookchainproject.com

Front cover image: gorodenkoff/iStock
Back cover images (clockwise from top right): courtesy FREITAG; courtesy
RAEBURN; courtesy Patagonia
Back flap images: courtesy Veja

Circular Fashion

MAKING THE FASHION
INDUSTRY SUSTAINABLE

PEGGY BLUM

Contents

INTRODUCTION: THE EVOLUTION OF THE FASHION INDUSTRY

A key form of self-expression, fashion is an important part of human culture and identity. It can signal to the world who we are or who we want to become. As a result, clothes have a big impact on our lives and on society as a whole. The creation and selling of fashion is now a huge business which comprises everything from design and development, to sourcing, logistics, retail, and marketing. Constantly advancing and adapting, this is an industry that prioritizes innovation, technological advancement, and creatively minded individuals.

However, the fashion industry as we know it today did not evolve until the late twentieth century. To understand the current state of the industry, it's important to consider how clothing production has changed over the last 300 years, morphing from handspun to digital, slow to fast, eventually becoming a trillion-dollar global enterprise.

THE DOMESTIC SYSTEM: 1300–1750

Prior to the mid-eighteenth century, many people in Western Europe and America spent their whole lives working, with the great majority laboring as farmers in the countryside. The agrarian society was characterized by the slow pace of the many and often labor-intensive tasks that had to be performed to maintain a household. The economic foundation of the agrarian society was a self-sufficient model with a barter exchange for goods of equal value or for produced goods.

In this society, families sewed their own clothing and made repairs to any garments that were ripped or worn out. Cloth was made from plant fibers such as flax, cotton, and hemp, as well as animal fibers such as wool and fur. The spinning

of fibers into threads for weaving cloth took place in homes. Most people owned a very limited amount of clothing because of the long time it took to produce. Individual handiwork was valued and people maintained clothes and possessions for years and even generations. Odd bits of

EARLY WARDROBE STAPLES

Smocks were a clothing staple of the agricultural workforce and the countryside's most distinctive garment. The earliest smocks were relatively plain and cut in a loose-fitting shape. They were made of fine bleached linen or coarser twill cotton and varied only in size. Many smocks were often made at home and handed down from one generation to another over a period of at least 50 years. Even so, there is evidence of a well-established trade of ready-made smocks from the early decades of the nineteenth century.[1]

cloth (rags) were repurposed into quilts or sold to merchants and peddlers who turned them into new goods. Production and disposal were one process, like a closed-loop system where materials are used and reused to create new products. Textile waste was minimal.

COTTAGE INDUSTRY

Alongside farming, a primary business in pre-industrial times was a home workshop, known as a "cottage industry." All family members who were able helped in the production of goods for sale such as food, clothing, furniture, and tools. Clothing was hand sewn, requiring time and skill.

> **Cottage industry: *a small business in which the work is done by people in their homes.***
> Oxford Learner's Dictionary

These small scale domestic systems (or "putting out systems") allowed rural families to increase their household income and merchants to take advantage of domestic labor by "putting-out" raw materials to the cottage industries for the manufacture of all types of goods including military uniforms, stockings, lace, shoes, and textiles.

It was not uncommon to see members of a family working alongside each other in one room. Hours were long but workers could take breaks for lunch or tend to children in the home. Workers were paid by "piecework," a fixed rate based on their output, and payment depended on the quality of the product. Different processes were generally carried out in several homes (typically cottages) as the materials or garments progressed from one stage to the next. Gender defined the kind of work a person did: men grew and harvested the plants, women and girls spun the fibers, and men then wove and took the cloth to the marketplace.

However, as the eighteenth century progressed, the slower production methods of the cottage industries struggled to keep pace with an ever-increasing population and a growing demand for clothing.

In 1783, William Hincks, a self-taught Irish portrait artist and engraver, published a series of 12 stipple engravings illustrating linen manufacturing. This engraving depicts a home where women are working: two women are spinning the yarn on a spindle Dutch (or low Irish) wheel, another woman is reeling the thread using a hexagonal frame, and a fourth woman is boiling the yarn in a large cauldron over a fire, poking it with a stick. A young boy is seated in the background. The scene is representative of a cottage industry where an entire family was involved in the process.

Simultaneously, inventors and entrepreneurs began working on methods and machines to improve production output, ultimately leading to the birth of mechanization, loss of rural employment, and the demise of the domestic system.

THE FACTORY SYSTEM: 1760–1830

New inventions and technologies in textile production began to emerge with the mechanization of spinning fiber into yarn. In 1764, James Hargreaves, an English weaver and carpenter, invented the "spinning jenny" which used eight different spindles powered by a single wheel. This allowed one worker to produce eight threads in the same amount of time it previously took to produce one thread. Shortly afterward, in 1769, Richard Arkwright patented his spinning frame, known as the "water frame," which allowed for large-scale spinning on one machine. Each machine required so much energy that it was built next to a river to utilize the force of the water to make it spin.

Another key development was Edmund Cartwright's power loom, first built in 1785. It was a steam-powered loom with foot pedals that lifted and then lowered the warp (vertical tighter threads) while the weft (horizontal weaker threads) were drawn between the warp to create cloth. This machine allowed for the more efficient and quicker production of textiles.

All of these inventions helped propel the transformation of British society from one centered on agriculture and handicraft to one dominated by industrialization and machines based on the factory system, a transformation known as the Industrial Revolution.

> **Industrial Revolution: *the period in the 18th and 19th centuries in Europe and the US when machines began to be used to do work, and industry grew rapidly.***
> Oxford Learner's Dictionary

The Industrial Revolution enabled the production of goods at a scale unprecedented in history. Clothing, shoes, tools, and

Textile workers at work in a northern mill in the US, 1800s.

household goods became more readily available and, as a result, less expensive. On a larger scale, foreign markets were created to sell these goods internationally, fueling the economies of industrialized nations and generating new wealth.

By the end of the eighteenth century, the technological developments in the textile industry that began in Britain spread to America. Eli Whitney's cotton-gin machine (patented in 1793) cleaned cotton of its seeds and replaced the slower manual removal of the seeds from the raw fiber. Samuel Slater, an Englishman, built a successful water-powered textile mill from memory in Pawtucket, Rhode Island in 1793. Known as the "father of the American factory

system," he is considered the founder of the American textile industry because the technology he brought with him began the Industrial Revolution there.

In Western Europe and America, the organization of newly developed factories, known as "manufactories," powered by steam to produce cloth and clothing, replaced rural industries. People who once worked at home, in a small shop or in the fields, migrated to the cities and took factory jobs working for large companies.

The working conditions were monotonous, dangerous, and unsanitary. Spinning machines posed the most serious risk, as moving parts often had no protective guard. Many workers were forced to work long hours for pitifully low wages. Children needed to work in order to help cover household costs and child labor was common.

The political ideology of the early nineteenth century was classical liberalism, which places emphasis on securing individual freedom with minimal or no government involvement. Therefore, governments did little to protect workers from exploitation by factory owners.

By the mid-nineteenth century, the introduction of the mechanized sewing machine by a trio of inventors—Walter Hunt, Elias Howe, and Isaac Singer—accelerated the pace of production, leading to an increased amount of goods being produced.

During this time, a specific type of factory also began to emerge in which a middleman, known as a "sweater," directed others in garment-making under a "sweating system" of arduous conditions. These workplaces were called "sweatshops."

Sweatshop: *a factory or workshop, especially in the clothing industry, where manual workers are employed at very low wages for long hours and under poor conditions.*
Oxford Dictionary

THE DAWN OF READY-TO-WEAR

As cloth became more readily available, manufacturers and merchants began producing and selling a new type of clothing that did not require a fitting but was made in standard sizes, known as "ready-to-wear," at affordable prices. Large mills and factories produced garments such as petticoats, shirts, trousers, gloves, and hats.

> *Ready-to-wear: clothing is made in a series of standard sizes, rather than made to fit the exact measurements of individual customers.*
>
> Collins English Dictionary

As industrialization progressed, a prosperous, urban middle class began to emerge. Skilled workers, managers, accountants, and clerks now had money left over for leisure goods.

In 1851, The Great Exhibition, held in the iconic Crystal Palace in London's Hyde Park, aimed to show that the industrial world was the key to a better future. Six million visitors were treated to an enormous showcase of technology, demonstrations of new inventions, and consumer goods from around the world. The exhibition projected an aura of excitement and influenced visitors in all matters of modernity—taste, culture, and fashion.

Crowds view the latest inventions at The Great Exhibition, Crystal Palace, 1851.

Inspired by the architecture of the Great Exhibition, particularly the use of vast panes of glass, and by its interior and visual arrangement, cloth merchants and entrepreneurs began to open department stores in major cities.

Department store: *a large shop that is divided into several parts, each selling different types of goods.*
Oxford Learner's Dictionary

The first was Le Bon Marché in Paris in 1852, with Macy's in New York following in 1858, and Selfridges in London in 1909. The stores offered a vast array of mass-produced goods for a public increasingly keen on consumption.

The presentation of shopping as a pleasurable leisure activity made department stores distinctive and represented a new opportunity for fashionable middle- and upper-class women to browse and shop freely, away from the home and the company of men. Stores encouraged a different kind of shopping experience, which was characterized by attractive displays and merchandise affixed with price tags. Many stores offered restaurants and tearooms to cater to women, encouraging them to view shopping as a social activity.

French couturiers such as Coco Chanel, Paul Poiret, and Madeline Vionnet came onto the scene in the early 1900s, quickly earning an international reputation as *the* arbiters of taste. Eager to capitalize on this fervor, American department stores sent their employees to France to covertly sketch Parisian runway designs, as it was legally permitted to copy these styles in the United States. Many department stores staged lavish presentations of their mass-produced "Paris Originals" alongside their own runway collections.

Knockoff: *a copy or imitation of something popular that sells for less than the original.*
Merriam-Webster Dictionary

The shift from tailor-made to ready-made clothing initiated the rapid rise of garment factories, as manufacturers took advantage of foreign labor. With little protection, working conditions steadily declined. These poor conditions tended to be worse in large cities where sweatshops could be hidden in slums. In 1911, the Triangle Shirtwaist Factory fire in New York City, in which 146 garment workers were killed, led to a public outcry that prompted new reform measures.

The 1920s and 1930s saw a proliferation of women's ready-to-wear clothing, as the rise of advertising, fashion magazines, mail order catalogs, and chain stores meant there was more clothing available to an ever-increasing number of people.

Importantly, the 1930s also saw the introduction of synthetic fibers: Nylon was developed in the 1930s by the chemical company Du Pont and was heralded as the first fully synthetic fiber. Nylon stockings, promoted as stronger and more affordable than silk stockings, were made commercially available in 1940 and proved an immediate hit.

As the twentieth century progressed, a rising middle class with increased purchasing power began to buy more mass-produced clothing in new, innovative synthetic fibers. In 1951, for instance, a clothing manufacturer in New York City introduced a men's summer suit marketed with the tagline "Miracles can happen." This revolutionary suit, which was more affordable and reportedly needed less care than those made from natural fibers, was made of a new synthetic fiber, Dacron polyester.[2]

Modern fashion is, therefore, inextricably linked to technological advancement. New ideas and innovations throughout history have shaped how we dress, changing the way clothes are created, manufactured, shipped, sold, and worn.

PLANNED OBSOLESCENCE

Some ideas are born from what is known as a "lightbulb moment," a breakthrough in thinking, an instance of clarity or of sudden realization. The lightbulb has long been a symbol of new ideas, human ingenuity, and innovation. Whenever a character in a comic or animation comes up with a new idea, a lightbulb appears over their head and illuminates. Voila! Something new is hatched.

In fact, the lightbulb, an everyday object we probably hardly give a second thought to when flipping the switch, illustrates one of the best and earliest examples of a design strategy commonly used in fashion: planned or built-in obsolescence. The lightbulb was originally invented in the first half of the nineteenth century and, as it developed throughout the rest of that century, the time it could last increased up to 2,500 hours. This innovation was good news for consumers, but not so good for lightbulb manufacturers. The longer lifespan of lightbulbs reduced consumer sales and profits steadily declined.

In 1925, lightbulb manufacturers formed a cartel and gathered for a meeting in Switzerland to discuss this serious threat to their industry.

It was then that they came to a collective decision to limit the lifespan of any lightbulb to 1,000 hours. The manufacturers instructed their designers and engineers to develop new lightbulbs with this shorter lifespan. As a result of their efforts, "new and improved" 1,000 hour lightbulbs were produced and introduced to the consumer market. Sales increased as consumers continuously purchased replacement lightbulbs and eventually profits steadily climbed. By limiting and standardizing the lifespan of lightbulbs, the cartel had enabled the deliberate obsolescence of their products.[3]

OVER 130 MILLION PAIRS OF TIGHTS ARE SOLD EVERY YEAR IN FRANCE.

The Halte à l'Obsolescence Programmée (HOP, "Stop Built-In Obsolescence") association polled over 3,000 women in 2018 to address the question: "Why did our grandmothers' tights seem more resistant than ours, which do not last?"

In the study, over two thirds (70%) of the women said that their tights generally lasted for only six uses before breaking or laddering and were then thrown away. Women were forced to buy up to 11 pairs of tights per season due to two factors: the low quality of the fabric and the use of additives that make the tights less durable.

France has made efforts to combat built-in obsolescence in consumer products. Following a government initiative rolled out in 2020, products will voluntarily be given a sticker on their packaging, indicating the expected durability of the product, and rate its repairability from 1 to 10. Could fashion be far behind?

Planned obsolescence: *a strategy of producing consumer goods that rapidly become obsolete and so require replacing, achieved by frequent changes in design, termination of the supply of spare parts, and the use of non-durable materials.*

Oxford English Dictionary

FAST FASHION

In the last decades of the twentieth century, fashion designers became like the lightbulb designers before them, developing clothes and accessories with limited lifespans. The Spanish fashion brand Zara, the flagship brand of Inditex, has been credited with introducing the first successful fast fashion business model in the early 1990s. The term "fast fashion" was used to describe the retailer's agile production model which takes as little as three weeks to go from runway sketch to new product on the retail floor. Today, Zara offers up to 20,000 new designs with new styles arriving in stores twice a week.[4]

Fast fashion: *an approach to the design, creation, and marketing of clothing fashions that emphasizes making fashion trends quickly and cheaply available to consumers.*

Merriam-Webster Dictionary

To compete with this new production model, many fashion brands began pushing a vast range of new styles at the expense of quality and sustainability. Compromises are often made along the supply chain.

Supply chain: *the entire process of making and selling commercial goods, including every stage from the supply of materials and the manufacture of the goods through to their distribution and sale.*

Collins Dictionary

Fast fashion is produced using low quality materials and poor construction techniques that are not designed for longevity. A study investigating the consumption habits of young fashion consumers found that fast-fashion items typically last no more than 10 wears.[5] It is clear that the mainstream or mass market fashion industry is intentionally creating clothing of inferior quality.

Sustainability: *the ability to continue or be continued for a long time and the use of natural products and energy in a way that does not harm the environment.*

Oxford Learner's Dictionary

In addition, brands have introduced fast fashion cycles in which colors, shapes, and styles change so frequently that consumers are made to feel that their clothes are out of style. In doing so, brands are increasing their profits by encouraging consumers to buy new items more frequently, even if the ones in their existing closets (wardrobes) are in excellent condition and perfectly serviceable.

Social media has also accelerated this insatiable appetite with daily offerings of real-time fashion and style trends from the runways (catwalks), the street, A-list celebrities, the red carpet, influencers, and more. Fashion Nova, a digital fast fashion brand, works with 1,000 manufacturers to introduce between 600 and 900 new styles every week. The brand has more than 17 million Instagram followers, with many users regularly posting selfies in the brand's trendy clothing.[6]

Fashion consumers who wish to be "on trend" and "in style" are encouraged through traditional and digital marketing platforms to make constant wardrobe replenishments. For example, a voluminous maxi dress will be "replaced" in the following season by a fitted mini skirt; slouchy trousers will appear "outdated" by skinny pants; green will look "old" next to blue. This built-in or planned obsolescence strategy puts an expiration date on fashion products. It creates a false sense of perishability before the garment has completed its full life cycle.

As we find ourselves in the third decade of the twenty first century, we know that as a society, our relationship to our clothing has radically changed. The increasing speed of our garment consumption, fueled by a reciprocal increase in the speed of low-cost fashion production and distribution, has resulted in waste and what is known as a "take-make-dispose" linear supply chain.

TAKE-MAKE-DISPOSE MODEL

Linear economy: a traditional economy model based on a "take-make-consume-throw away" approach of resources.
GEMET

The manufacturing model of built-in obsolescence is representative of a centuries-old economic system that began in the Industrial Revolution and is still in place today. It is a linear mindset driven by proprietary ownership of ideas and intellectual property (IP), and fueled by a production model that is hungry for resources and profits. The model is also wasteful along its supply chain.

Let's look at some of the environmental waste in two key areas of today's take-make-dispose linear model—manufacturing and the consumer.

MANUFACTURING WASTE

The oldest and most traditional form of clothing manufacturing is known as CMT (cut-make-trim). CMT factories produce garments from start-to-finish. They cut the fabric, sew the fabric, and attach any trimmings such as hangtags, buttons, labels, etc. Some CMT factories may subcontract elements of the work, but typically they manage the entire production process.

Pre-consumer waste is material waste generated in the manufacturing process of the supply chain before the product reaches the consumer—for example, leftover scraps of fabric or trimmings that end up on the factory floor. According to Reverse Resources, 25% of resources spill out of original supply chains for a variety of reasons. Even

THE LINEAR SUPPLY CHAIN

Less than 1% of material used to produce clothing is recycled

1 Inspiration/research → 2 Design → 3 Raw materials → 4 Manufacturing → 5 Distribution → 6 Retail → 7 Consumer

pre-consumer waste: 25% of resources gets spilled from factories

post-consumer waste: 73% of clothing ends up in landfills

though some of these materials get used elsewhere, most materials get downcycled, incinerated, or dumped.[7]

Downcycle: *to recycle (something) in such a way that the resulting product is of a lower value than the original item; to create an object of lesser value from a discarded object of higher value.*

Merriam-Webster Dictionary

CONSUMER WASTE

At the end of the linear supply chain, the consumer is responsible for the final part of the life cycle and disposal of garments. Post-consumer waste is material waste that's been used and disposed of by a consumer. An estimated value of $500 billion (£385 billion) is lost every year due to clothing being barely worn and rarely recycled. According to the Copenhagen Fashion Summit's Pulse of the Fashion Industry report in 2017, the fashion industry is responsible for 92 million tons (tonnes) of solid waste per year globally, representing 4% of the 2.12 billion tons of waste that end in landfills globally each year.[8]

Post-consumer: *(of a consumer item) having been discarded for disposal or recovery.*

Collins Dictionary

Supply chain problems don't end with the squandering of precious resources such as water, energy, nature, and animals, or the physical waste that fails to biodegrade in landfills. It also extends to the people and the time spent creating clothing that producers and consumers of fashion obtain and discard so easily. Consumers are increasingly disconnected from the workers making their clothes. Approximately 60 million people are employed in the fashion value chain, many of whom are women who do not enjoy fair employment rights, nor do they share in the prosperity of their employers, the world's most profitable fashion brands.

A new economic system is needed to rethink every step along the supply chain from land and resource use to the design, properties, and end use of materials. It may seem daunting at first to think about all the challenges we face, but if we start by asking ourselves a few questions, and then have a discussion with others around us, we may begin to see a shift in our collective thinking.

THINK PIECE:
How can we challenge ourselves to think more deeply about the products we create, the waste we generate, and our own clothing consumption habits?

GOT 10 SECONDS?

"Every second, the equivalent of one garbage truck of textiles is landfilled or burned."[9]

Part 1
Create

01:
A CIRCULAR MINDSET

As we begin to question what kind of fashion industry we aspire to, a new mindset will be the catalyst to create this desirable future. It requires a new way of thinking, a new set of assumptions, methods, or beliefs that foster sustainability as an integral part of the industry's ethos.

THE CIRCLE GAME

For a moment, imagine a circle. Mathematically, you might be thinking of a round plane whose circumference consists of points at equal distances. Or perhaps you visualize something or someone moving all the way around more than once: for example, "we circled all around the globe—twice." If you imagined either or both of these, then you imagined the right thing. Circles are models of all possibilities since the circle has no beginning or end.

The circle is a powerful universal symbol that plays an important role in the iconography of several religions. In Buddhism, for instance, circles often form philosophical symbols that correspond with the cyclical nature of birth, life, death, and rebirth, constantly spiraling in a loop. As a wheel turns, the center remains still while everything else moves around it.

Scientists study circles in the form of atoms, molecules, planets, orbits, the sun, and the moon. Artists like Alexander Calder and Wassily Kandinsky have painted circles, while musicians like Joni Mitchell have sung about them. Some psychologists even suggest that we associate shapes with our emotions, and that circles correspond with our happiness.

Most important, many processes in nature are circular, occurring in cycles (from the Greek *kyklos* for circle or wheel) or parts of cycles which are efficient in the minimization of energy and resource waste. These cycles enable many processes and organisms to be essentially at equilibrium but always changing.

NATURE: A CIRCULAR SYSTEM

As a perfect circular system, nature is, therefore, an inspiring model for the fashion industry. The four seasons—spring, summer, fall (autumn), and winter—follow each other in a never-ending cycle. Every season is characterized generally by its own distinct amount of light, temperature, and weather patterns. The seasonal cycle also has an enormous influence on the growth of plants and the reproduction of animals. There is no landfill in the natural world. Plants absorb sunlight, animals eat plants and other animals. After dying, both plants and animals decompose into nutrients of biomolecules and minerals, becoming part of the next generation.

Woodland constantly changes over time through a cyclical process called "succession." Each stage lays the groundwork for the next cycle. The first stage begins with bare soil, perhaps an abandoned field, and the next stages see the trees grow from seed to seedling, then on to maturity and eventually death and decomposition as the forest evolves. If a disturbance occurs such as a fire, the forest recovers from the damage by slowly restoring itself back to its former state.[10]

Biomimicry is an approach to innovation that seeks sustainable solutions to human challenges by emulating nature's time-tested patterns and strategies. The goal is to create products, processes, and policies—new ways of living—that are well-adapted to life on earth over the long haul.[11] The core idea is that what surrounds us in nature is the secret to human survival. For example, learning from termites how to create sustainable buildings or reimaging forests as factories.

Biomimicry relies on three key principles:

1. Nature as model: Study nature's models and then emulate these forms, processes, systems, and strategies to solve human problems.
2. Nature as measure: Use an ecological standard to judge the sustainability of our innovations.
3. Nature as mentor: View and value nature based not on what we can extract from the natural world, but on what we can learn from it.[12]

LEARNING FROM NATURE

Fashion is highly dependent on nature's resources for its existence. Our clothing is produced using fabrics created from plants (cotton, linen, rayon), animals (leather, silk), and petroleum (polyester and acrylic). Farmers plow fields, plant seeds, use water, fertilizer, and pesticides so we can wear our favorite cotton T-shirt. Food is grown to feed the animals that are used to make leather shoes, handbags, and belts. Petroleum is extracted from the earth to produce synthetic

Above: John Baldessari captures circular thinking perfectly in *Not Harper's Bazaar*, 2015.

fibers, and also to transport materials and clothing to homes and retail stores.

The world's stock of natural assets, which include not only all living things but also soil, air, and water, is referred to as "natural capital."[13] As human needs expand and consumer demand for clothing increases, pressures mount on both renewable and non-renewable natural capital, and the need to restore and regenerate these resources increases.

To address this need there are two important ways in which circular fashion follows nature's lead: by being regenerative and restorative. "Regenerative" means to regrow or replace something, and "restorative" to reinstate it to its right place. The choice of material can play an important role in circular fashion, lessening the negative impact on the environment. Regenerative and restorative agriculture practices can also reduce the environmental damage by rebuilding the soil and restoring degraded soil biodiversity. For instance, growing hemp prevents soil erosion, acts as a natural pest and weed repellent, and requires very little water. As a material choice, hemp provides excellent durability and biodegradable properties.

CIRCULAR FASHION

The concept of circular fashion is easily understood by comparing a line and a circle. A line is defined as a straight path that is endless in both directions. Consider the line in a linear fashion system (see page 14). Now, imagine all the resources we use along that line, such as the materials to create the clothing you wear, the packaging and shopping bags to take these items home, and even the remnants you no longer wear in your closet. After some time, and when we have finished with these things, we simply discard them. In other words, we consume, then use these resources up over and over endlessly. These discarded materials pile up and may become waste in landfills or in the natural environment.

Now, consider turning this line into a circle where materials are responsibly sourced, clothes are designed for longevity with the intention that they stay circulated for their full life cycle, and when no longer in use are restored back to the earth, becoming a valuable resource for future products.

"Circular fashion" can be defined as clothes, shoes, or accessories that are designed, sourced, produced, and provided with the intention to be used and circulated responsibly and effectively in society for as long as possible in their most valuable form, and hereafter returned safely to the biosphere when no longer of human use.
Dr. Anna Brismar, 2017, Green Strategy[14]

Once you understand how each component of the circular fashion model interconnects with natural resources, people, and the planet, while capturing new economic opportunities, you will see how this change from a line to a circle is the most natural fit for our fashion future.

A CIRCULAR FASHION MODEL

A "circle of responsibility" is the accountability, traceability, and ownership of the entire life cycle of a product—from the seeds and the fibers, design and materials, dyes and finishes, manufacturing and remanufacturing, to the workers in the factories, transportation, and packaging, and how the customer might repair, renew, or resell the product.

A "circular fashion model" conveys a circle of responsibility along its supply chain that is vital for all producers of fashion apparel and accessories. A circle of responsibility unites the whole fashion system with one common goal—designing, producing, and consuming clean, safe, and ethical apparel:

CREATE

Design is key in the shift to a circular fashion model, which requires greater focus on doing things "right from the start." Designers need to think of themselves as co-creators of intentionally designed garments made for durability, disassembly, recycling, and biodegradability. A system of design mutuality continuously asks: "What is it that we want to circulate?" and ensures a circle of responsibility prevails around each product. As positive change agents, designers share stories of proof of concept along with trial and error to bring circular design to life.

Proof of concept: the stage during the development of a product when it is established that the product will function as intended.
Collins Dictionary

MAKE

Human-centric, digitized communities create a circle of responsibility around people and processes. Access to new innovations and technologies that design out waste, increase the share of recycled fibers, reduce water consumption, and eliminate the use of toxic chemicals should be utilized in production. Respectful, safe, and secure work environments, alongside training and upskilling, are components of a new factory system. Reliable wage systems promote prosperity and well-being for the workforce.

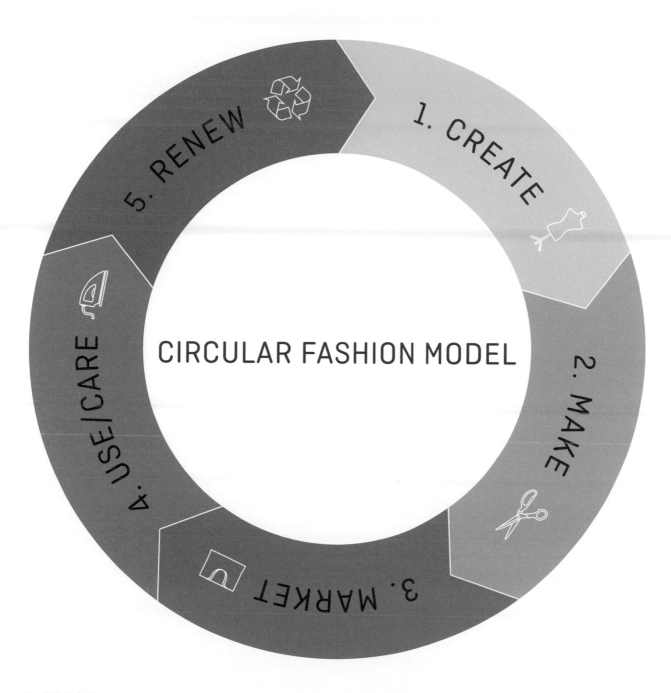

CIRCULAR FASHION MODEL

1. CREATE

2. MAKE

3. MARKET

4. USE/CARE

5. RENEW

Circularity in fashion requires
transformation in every aspect
of its value chain.

MARKET

Cross-industry collaboration focuses on renewable energy, clean transport, and environmentally friendly packaging designs. The profit and loss financial methods and investments used must take into account the environmental health of an organization and its impact in creating, making, and marketing garments for sale. Store lighting, design, and merchandising models should move to zero impact. Narratives of integrity and authenticity sell circular products to consumers.

USE/CARE/REPAIR

Product life cycle assessments (PLA) examine every phase of a garment's life and adjust processes to achieve minimal environmental impact. Garment warranties and easy self-repair kits are issued by producers and adhere to quality, environmental, and longevity standards. Customers participate in a circle of responsibility through smart consumption habits and transition from garment ownership to rental or service-oriented models to gain access to fashion products. Citizen-driven, community-oriented repair cafés inspire circularity at a local level.

RENEW

International industry information exchanges, new technologies and infrastructure, standards and governance for collection and processing, and multi-stakeholder funding and initiatives generate a global circle of responsibility to eliminate textile waste. Second- and even third-generation garments mixed with first-generation waste go back around the system, as efforts to collect materials from end-of-life clothes are maximized.

CHANGING THE MINDSET

When a system has been in place for as long as the linear system, habits and routines are embedded. People working in the fashion industry may have learned to do things one way, without questioning their legitimacy or considering more efficient methods, while consumers purchasing fashion goods may have become accustomed to low prices, an abundance of trendy styles, and frequent updates.

Educating and inspiring all stakeholders to gain a fresh perspective on their current methods, practices, or processes and open up to new ways of working and consuming fashion is of paramount importance.

Stakeholder: a person such as an employee, customer, or citizen who is involved with an organization, society, etc. and therefore has responsibility towards it and an interest in its success.
Cambridge Dictionary

CONSUMER MINDSET

Consumers look to fashion brands for education, information, and a common language when it comes to circularity and sustainability. They are increasingly interested in how brands communicate these messages on websites, social media, and through advertising, and also look for third party certifications and labels to verify the brand's claims. When out shopping, consumers might also look for hang tags, signage, packaging, and informed sales associates to guide them toward more sustainable product choices.

However, while many surveys seemingly report that consumers want ethical and sustainable products, many are still unwilling to pay for the extra costs associated with them. A 2019 report from the e-commerce platform Nosto indicated that of the 2,000 US- and UK-based shoppers surveyed, 52% wanted the fashion industry to follow sustainable practices, but only 29% would pay more for sustainably made versions of the same clothing items.[15]

Traditional rational models of consumer behavior indicate that individuals make purchasing decisions which balance the cost of the product against its benefits. Sustainable, ethical consumers make these rational judgements of cost and benefit, while also seeing the impact of their purchase on the world, the environment, and their health. Fashion consumption, however, is based on an irrational model, driven by pleasure, desire, and excitement. This fosters a less rational approach to consumption where desire may quash the influence of rational purchasing decisions about sustainability, ethics, and environmental consequences.

Fashion brands must help change this mindset by creating exciting fashion products with built-in sustainable solutions but without the added costs. To do this it is essential that brands embrace sustainability as an organizational change, utilizing new technologies and business models to overcome technical and commercial challenges.

INDUSTRY MINDSET

Organizational change toward more sustainable and circular processes will take some time and, for it to be effective, there will be a transition period.

A circular system must be looked upon as an investment in terms of resource allocation and time. The implementation of new methods, processes, and practices may cause uncertainty, even chaos in the short term, but this is necessary to gain long-term efficiency and positive environmental impact. If the change is to be successful, it must be made permanent or become standard operating procedure.

SYSTEMS THINKING

Moving toward a circular fashion model requires a collaborative mindset—a multidisciplinary way of seeing and talking about current processes or practices and recognizing the interrelatedness of things. Systems thinking contrasts with traditional problem analysis, which studies systems by breaking them down into their separate elements.

> *Systems thinking is the process of understanding how component parts of a system can best be understood in the context of relationships with each other and other systems, rather than in isolation. Systems thinking focuses on cyclical rather than linear cause and effect.*
> Ellen MacArthur Foundation, ellenmacarthurfoundation.org

Using systems thinking allows us to look at problems not as isolated challenges but in the context of the larger network in which an activity or process operates. For example, a material purchasing decision in an organization is not just about material cost, lead time, and quality, but also about production cost, flexibility of time, and product longevity as well as the overall financial management of the firm. Therefore, a purchasing decision relates to the whole system within the organization.

THE CIRCULAR ECONOMY

A circular fashion model is just one part of a larger system, known as the Circular Economy, a global economic system that has deep-rooted origins in many schools of thought that were instrumental in its development since the 1970s.

> *A Circular Economy (CE) is an economic system where products and services are traded in closed loops or cycles. A circular economy is characterized as an economy which is regenerative by design, with the aim to retain as much value as possible of products, parts, and materials.*
> Kraaijenhagen, Van Oppen & Bocken, 2016[16]

A common understanding of the Circular Economy from the following perspectives will help businesses and organizations in the fashion industry successfully implement change.

CRADLE TO CRADLE

Walter Stahel, architect and industrial analyst, is credited with having coined the expression "Cradle to Cradle" in the late 1970s. From the 1990s, Michael Braungart and William McDonough developed the Cradle to Cradle™ concept and certification process (see page 147). This design philosophy aims to eliminate the concept of waste, use renewable energy, and respect human and natural systems. The concept differentiates between biological and technical nutrient cycles and states that product components should be designed for continuous restoration and regeneration, recovery and reutilization within a biological or technical cycle.[17]

CIRCULAR ECONOMY MODEL

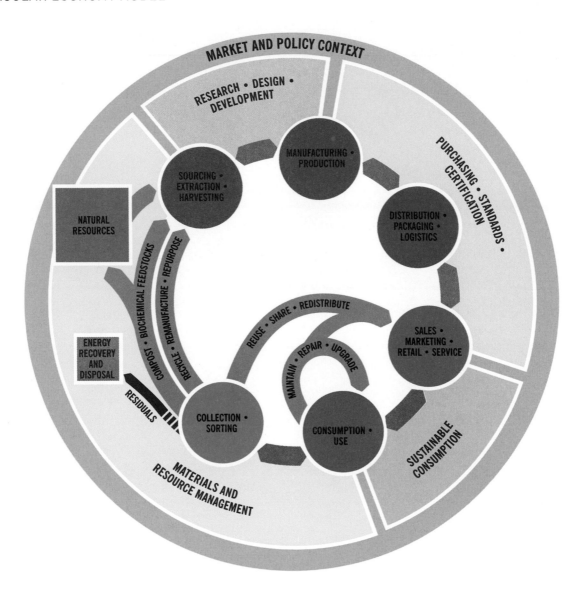

This diagram shows how paper and packaging materials and products move through a circular economy. The outer circle represents the wide-ranging government and market policies that influence decision making, while the inner circle shows the life cycle stages of paper and packaging products. The green loops indicate a variety of pathways for closing the loop after consumption or first use.

Cradle to Cradle principles in action: The Adidas x Parley partnership makes commercially successful products from reclaimed ocean plastic.

PERFORMANCE ECONOMY

Walter Stahel worked at developing a "closed-loop" approach to production processes and created the Product Life Institute in Geneva in 1982. This institute pursues four main goals: product-life extension, long-life goods, reconditioning activities, and waste prevention. Based on these goals Stahel developed the "performance economy" concept. This is an economic model which seeks to reduce environmental impact by selling services instead of goods.[18]

Closed loop: of or pertaining to a processing system in which effluents are recycled, that is, treated or returned for reuse.
WordReference

INDUSTRIAL ECOLOGY

Industrial ecology is a framework for environmental management of industrial systems which aims to reduce the environmental impact of industry by closing material loops in products, processes, industrial sectors, and economies.

NATURAL CAPITALISM

"Natural capital" is harnessing the world's stock of natural resources including air, water, soil, and all living things as business assets with enormous economic value. In their book *Natural Capitalism: Creating the Next Industrial Revolution*, Paul Hawken, Amory Lovins, and L. Hunter Lovins posit that an economic system where business and environmental interests overlap can simultaneously satisfy customers' needs, increase profits, and solve environmental issues.[19]

Designer Isabel Fletcher closes the loop by using discarded materials made from wool, hemp, linen, and bamboo in her collections. The buttons here are made from potato waste (Parblex—see page 69).

CIRCULAR LEADERS

Successfully shifting to a circular fashion model means redefining leadership to align with new social, environmental, and economic principles. It means building new communities with people at all levels of industry, inside and outside organizations, and in all types of sectors across the globe. It requires collaborative leaders to shape new mindsets.

Purpose-driven leaders know the people working for them, their skill set, and perhaps even something more about what makes them who they are. As stakeholders in their business, they are less focused on the number of products produced and more concerned about what those products are produced with.

As leaders of an industry in transition, key players must develop a circular mindset that reflects a sense of humanity and a genuine concern for the planet. These will be the driving forces behind the new paradigm.

THINK PIECE:
How can we change mindsets so that we can all live a more sustainable life, and so life here on this planet can continue?

CIRCULAR LEADER:
DAME ELLEN MACARTHUR

Dame Ellen MacArthur made yachting history in 2005, when she became the fastest solo sailor to circumnavigate the globe. She remains the UK's most successful offshore racer ever, having won the Ostar and the Route du Rhum, and finished second in the Vendée Globe. She received the French Legion of Honour from President Nicolas Sarkozy in 2008, three years after having been made a Dame by HM Queen Elizabeth II.

Having become acutely aware of the finite nature of the resources on which our linear economy relies, she retired from professional sailing to launch the Ellen MacArthur Foundation in 2010. The Foundation works to accelerate the transition to a circular economy and has helped put the subject on the agenda of decision makers around the world. Since the publication of its first economic report in 2012, the Foundation has launched global initiatives on plastics and textiles, developed innovation networks with educators, businesses, and governments, and released almost 20 further reports and books. Dame Ellen is a World Economic Forum Global Agenda Trustee for Environment and Natural Resource Security and a member of its Platform for Accelerating the Circular Economy. She sat on the European Commission's Resource Efficiency Platform between 2012 and 2014.

With the aim "to create a system that delivers benefits for citizens, the environment, and businesses,"[20] The Make Fashion Circular initiative united the Ellen MacArthur Foundation with fashion producers, designers, and brands behind the following three key principles:

Business models that keep clothes in use
Materials that are renewable and safe
Solutions that turn used clothes into new clothes

(ellenmacarthurfoundation.org)

02: DESIGN THINKING AND RE-THINKING

Transitioning to circular fashion design is one of the greatest challenges of our century. While many brands already see circular design as an essential component of a long-term circular business strategy, more needs to be done. For designers, it means rethinking traditional approaches, retraining in new circular methods, and sharing knowledge about circular design practices.

TRADITIONAL DESIGN THOUGHT

Today's fashion designers apply personal knowledge, inspiration, and design theories blended with research from trend forecasting services, trade reports, and market analysis to create a range of seasonally determined apparel and accessories known as a "fashion collection." These collections have traditionally followed a set calendar divided into four seasons: Spring-Summer, Fall-Winter, Resort (also called "Cruise"), and Pre-Fall. The two most important fashion seasons are Spring-Summer and Fall-Winter. The Spring-Summer collections arrive in January and appear until June in retail stores, while the Fall-Winter collections arrive in July and appear until December.

Every fashion collection is replaced by a new collection each season. Style trends for a season are introduced at biannual fashion weeks that also follow a set calendar, taking place several months before the season (usually September for Spring-Summer and February for Fall-Winter). These fashion weeks are traditionally held in New York, London, Milan, and

Paris, though this jet-setting program will need to be reappraised in light of COVID-19 and increasing criticism of such an environmentally damaging practice.

For a long time, the fashion calendar made sense. Runway shows enabled buyers and the press to preview new styles that would generally be available to consumers in six months' time. This gave magazine editors and retailers time to plan their fashion content and make buying decisions.

Since the advent of a faster fashion cycle, consumers are increasingly impatient with the lengthy lead times of the traditional cycle and are opting for a "buy now, wear now" ethos, even in the luxury markets. To meet this demand designers are ignoring the traditional fashion calendar of four seasons in favor of a seasonless model, "dropping" capsule collections, or even just a few items, to avoid appearing irrelevant in the consumer's mind.

Historically, fashion designers were the influencers of their day. Fashion was generally organized in accordance with the trickle-down theory of fashion adoption: For a style to be identified as a true fashion, it must first be adopted by the people at the upper echelons of society. Celebrities, royalty, and socialites were always the first to wear the new styles, and gradually those styles gained acceptance among lower socio-economic groups. Ultimately, as the styles became more popular, the affluent rejected them and replaced them with newer styles produced every season.

Since the birth of the internet and the meteoric rise of social media, there has been an unprecedented shift in fashion design theory. Today, the influencers are those promoting trends on Instagram and other social media platforms. New style trends appear in "real time" from the runway, and these style trends gain an almost immediate acceptance by consumers of all socio-economic levels as they are quickly duplicated by designers or the influencers themselves. Speed-to-market acceleration has become ubiquitous in the marketplace and, together with built-in obsolescence, problematic from a sustainability perspective.

Driven by data which indicates that current industry practices are environmentally harmful, a radical movement of more thoughtful design practices is now gaining traction. Fashion designers as activists, such as Vivienne Westwood and Stella McCartney, are asking different questions, engaging in peer-to-peer conversations, and anticipating future challenges that may ultimately change fashion design processes, but may also change what designing fashion means.[21]

DESIGN THINKING

Thinking about ways to introduce often complex sustainable and circular processes, principles, and mindsets can be unsettling. However, there are methodologies that can help guide designers away from traditional design approaches and toward innovation.

Design thinking, as in the notion of design as a way of thinking, comprises various processes that may help foster creative problem solving. As shown in the following example, reframing thinking by asking different questions is key.

> **Design thinking: *a human-centered approach to innovation that draws from the designer's toolkit to integrate the needs of people, the possibilities of technology, and the requirements for business success.***
>
> Tim Brown, CEO of IDEO, ideou.com

One of the most important tools in garment construction is a good pair of scissors. Using the wrong scissors can damage the fabric and make a job much harder. If asked to design a better pair of scissors to cut fabric, you may immediately think of improving the two metal blades attached to a comfortable handle. But if asked instead to simply design a better way to cut fabric, you might imagine something more compact with a single blade or something more versatile with a rotating blade that cuts not only fabric but also, say, a homemade pizza. Traditional problem solving starts with a solution already in mind, while design thinking focuses on the problem.

As influential global design firm IDEO founder David Kelley says, design thinking is not a linear path: "it's a big mass of looping back to different places in the process."[22] To illustrate this point let's examine the thought process of a designer at the forefront of sustainable design. A lifelong vegetarian, Stella McCartney knew that she didn't want to use animal products in her luxury brand, so the question became what eco-friendly alternatives would allow her to create similarly luxurious finishes. When her brand was launched in 2001 with an ethos of no animal-based textiles, not using animal products was pretty much unheard of in the fashion industry. Using eco-friendly alternatives, however, turned out to be a smart move in design thinking.

THE PRINCIPLES OF DESIGN THINKING

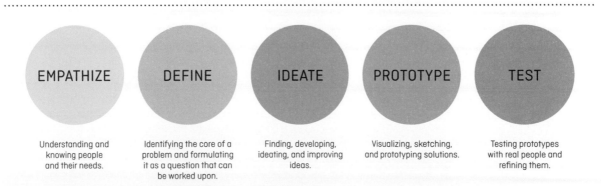

EMPATHIZE	DEFINE	IDEATE	PROTOTYPE	TEST
Understanding and knowing people and their needs.	Identifying the core of a problem and formulating it as a question that can be worked upon.	Finding, developing, ideating, and improving ideas.	Visualizing, sketching, and prototyping solutions.	Testing prototypes with real people and refining them.

CIRCULAR LEADER:
STELLA McCARTNEY

Raised on an organic farm in the English countryside, Stella McCartney has a love for the natural world which forms the foundation of her work as a successful sustainable fashion designer.

McCartney's interest in designing clothing began at a very young age. At 13, she constructed her own jacket, igniting a passion that eventually led to the prestigious art and design college Central Saint Martins, in London. She graduated in 1995, having sold her entire final student collection to Tokio, an influential London fashion boutique. In 1997, McCartney succeeded Karl Lagerfeld as creative director of French fashion house Chloé. By 2001, she had gained enough confidence to start her own eponymous label.

Stella McCartney was committed to sustainability long before it became fashionable to be so. A lifelong vegetarian, she is a pioneer of animal welfare, never using animal fur in her collections

and developing innovative substitutes for animal-based materials. McCartney is also a member of the Sustainable Apparel Coalition, an organization which sets science-based environmental goals, such as reducing greenhouse gas emissions and eliminating hazardous chemicals in the textile, footwear, and apparel industries. Since 2004, her partnership with Adidas has introduced high-fashion technical activewear in eco-friendly materials and sustainable footwear, such as vegan Stan Smith trainers, to a wider audience.

All Stella McCartney offices and stores in the UK are powered by wind energy and have recycling systems. As the fashion industry's conscience, McCartney balances creating luxurious clothing with an innate sense of responsibility for the resources she uses and the impact they have on the environment and all its creatures.

Notice how the following steps helped McCartney with her design thinking, by identifying solutions to key challenges that ultimately supported her brand's core principles:

1. **Empathize:** Empathy is at the heart of all human-centered design. As a designer, the problems you are trying to solve are usually those of a particular group of people. Gaining insight through observation or engaging with people directly will guide you in understanding the needs of those you are designing for and what those needs represent to them.

    Stella McCartney has built her company on a solid understanding of her own and her customer's environmental beliefs and values. Based on sustainable fashion ethics that resonate with her core customer base, her vegan collection does not use any animal-based textiles including leather, fur, skins, and feathers.

2. **Define:** Through analysis, you can begin to synthesize the information learned during the empathy phase in order to identify a problem. From there, a meaningful and actionable problem statement, or description of the issue to be addressed, is developed in a human-centric manner.

    McCartney has defined the problem to be solved in these terms: "The consumption of animals, whether you're wearing them or eating them, is extraordinarily damaging to the planet. There are over a billion animals killed a year for food, half of which don't even get eaten. And there's over 50 million animals killed just for fashion."[23] With this knowledge, she was able to ask the question: "What is the alternative?"

3. **Ideate:** This is a transition stage from identifying problems to finding solutions through to designing with your imagination. Ideas generated in this stage may be "out

Fur-free-fur at Stella McCartney's
Spring Summer (Resort) 2020
presentation, Milan, 2019.

4. **Prototype:** This experimental phase aims to identify a solution. Several inexpensive, scaled-down versions of the product or specific features found within the product are shared and tested and either accepted, improved, or rejected.

   A case in point is McCartney's decision to try out an alternative to fur in her collection: "The decision to include faux fur in our designs [...] has not been made without much debate [...] Ultimately, we concluded that by offering a luxury Fur-Free-Fur product that is such a good alternative to real fur we are demonstrating no animal needs to be harmed for fashion."[24]

5. **Test:** This is an opportunity to solicit feedback from the people you are designing for or users of your product. Sometimes it means going back to the drawing board while other times it yields unexpected results.

   McCartney solicits feedback from her customers to support her decision to use the faux fur alternative. "Modern fake fur looks so much like real fur, that the moment it leaves the atelier no one can tell it's not the real thing, and I've struggled with that. But I've been speaking to younger women about it recently and they don't even want real fur. So, I feel like maybe things have moved on [...] and we can do fabrics which look like fur."[25]

The design thinking process puts the user at the heart of all activities from start to finish. Suppose nature was also put at the heart of all the activities from start to finish? How do you design with nature? For example, empathizing with nature as we would people or animals, using nature to define a problem, ideating by looking at nature for inspiration, prototyping nature and technology, and testing based on nature's potential to provide solutions.

The beauty of the design thinking methodology is that it gives everyone an opportunity to participate in the process and see the bigger picture toward circularity initiatives within and outside an organization. Design thinking can help widen the focus from the product to material flows, production processes and conditions, and aspects of use and reuse, while also offering a better understanding of human and ecological principles.

of the box" or "going wide" as you look at alternative ways to view the problem.

McCartney has invested consistently in finding alternative solutions and introducing sustainable materials that have brought changes to the entire industry; from "skin-free-skin" leather alternatives to "fur-free-fur" and recycled marine plastic, as well as partnering with technology innovator Bolt Threads on yeast-based silk.

CIRCULAR FASHION DESIGN CONSIDERATIONS

Circular fashion design can bring creativity and magic back into fashion by imagining new and innovative products that are safe and healthy for ourselves and the planet. But it may mean going back to the drawing board to think hard about this work.

LONGEVITY IN DESIGN

Designing clothing with longevity in mind focuses on prolonging the lifespan of a garment, reducing the need to consume or replace clothing items so frequently. In an era of disposable fashion, most consumers discard their clothes because they no longer remain in style or look good. Timeless clothing styles, on the other hand, withstand seasons and trends by appealing to consumers for many years to come.

If designers are to create something that lasts, there also has to be a certain amount of time and love, as well as skill, going into the process.

SLOW DESIGN

"Slow design" is a philosophy that supports designers in developing their projects at the right time and the right speed, so that they can reflect carefully upon their actions. It is as much about material choices and thoughtfulness and deliberation in the design purpose, as it is about skills.

According to Amsterdam-based Slow Research Lab, there are six principles of slow design:

1. **Reveal:** Everyday life experiences that are often missed or forgotten, including the materials and processes that can be easily overlooked in an artifact's creation, are discovered.
2. **Expand:** The real and potential "expressions" of an

Variations of the iconic trench coat on display at Burberry, Covent Garden, London.

artifact and its environment beyond their perceived functionality, physical attributes, and lifespans are considered.

3. **Reflect:** Artifacts/environments/experiences induce contemplation and what has been coined "reflective consumption."

4. **Engage:** Open-source and collaborative processes, relying on sharing, cooperation, and transparency of information, are used so that designs may continue to evolve into the future.

5. **Participate:** Users are encouraged to become active participants in the design process, embracing ideas of conviviality and exchange to foster social accountability and enhance communities.

6. **Evolve:** Richer experiences can emerge from the dynamic maturation of artifacts, environments, and systems over time, so it is important to look beyond the needs and circumstances of the present day.[26]

Slow fashion: a term which describes clothing which lasts a long time and is often made from locally sourced or fair-trade material.
Macmillan Dictionary

Designing fashion with a slow design approach is about creating clothing that consumers treasure and want to keep because it has an inherent quality. It is about clothing with enduring meaning and value. Slow fashion design aims to establish the longevity of a garment and a lifelong relationship between the user and the garment.

DURABILITY IN DESIGN

Extending the life of clothing by an extra nine months in the United Kingdom (UK) would reduce carbon, waste, and water footprints by around 20% to 30% each, and cut resource costs by 20% or £5 billion ($6.5 billion).[27] To achieve these savings, we need longer-lasting clothes. The durability of a garment is measured by meaningful design: how long the item provides a functional service to the user and the degree of emotional attachment the user has to the garment. In order to design a long-lasting garment, both functional and emotional durability must be present.

Functional durability

Quality underlies all other factors when designing clothing because without quality, the true value and durability of the clothing is reduced. Designing for durability places emphasis on the construction of the garment, material choices, and manufacturing processes.

Successful durable clothing design is the result of designers matching the right colors, materials, finishes, and product features to a particular end-use or range of activities. For instance, Thomas Burberry's choice of a water-resistant and windproof gabardine fabric proved essential for protecting soldiers in the trenches during World War I and for stylish fashion consumers today.

Easy, correct, and precise care instructions for specific garments also enable users to participate in extending the life of their clothing.

Emotional durability

The connection between a consumer and an item of clothing also plays a prominent role in designing for durability. A garment's comfort, fit, or how it wears over time determines whether it is discarded or kept and cared for by the consumer. UK menswear designer Tom Cridland uses a special treatment to protect his classic, luxury-inspired sweatshirts and T-shirts against shrinking, and also offers a 30-year merchandise guarantee. If the garment shrinks, or is in need of any repair, it will be replaced or repaired for free.[28] This commitment on the part of the designer communicates to consumers that this is an item to care for long-term, not casually discard.

REPAIRABILITY IN DESIGN

Originating in Japan, wabi-sabi is a way of living that focuses on finding beauty within the imperfections of life and accepting peacefully the natural cycle of growth and decay. A wabi approach to fashion design is therefore one that considers how clothing can be repaired after natural wear and tear, and how through that process the clothing gains another chapter in its story, or an opportunity to embrace its imperfection.

Left: Japanese Sashiko Jacket from the Meiji period (1868–1912), comprising indigo-dyed plain-weave cotton, embroidered with white cotton thread.

Right: Boro patched jacket by KUON, Tokyo.

Wabi-sabi: *a Japanese concept that involves recognizing the beauty in transience and imperfection.*

Macmillan Dictionary

For example, until the late nineteenth century, people in rural Japan mastered repair techniques with their boro patchworked garments mended in sashiko stitching. Sashiko translates as "little stabs"—a reference to the plain running stitch that makes up the geometric, all-over patterns of the technique. Boro, meaning "ragged" or "tattered," garments grew out of economic necessity for the families of rural farmers and peasants wishing to extend the life of their clothing over generations.

Boro: *Japanese, a textile or garment that has been repeatedly patched or mended.*

Susan Brown and Matilda McQuaid[29]

Another example of inspired repairing can be found in the 1940s and 1950s. The rationing of materials imposed during World War II impacted on the clothing industry and led to a resurgence of mending out of economic necessity. The "Make-do and Mend" ethos thrived in the UK and was promoted as a patriotic duty through numerous pamphlets, posters, and magazines that shared tips and techniques on how to repair materials and make old clothing look new again.

Today, the make-do and mend ethos has gained popularity in communities, with free meeting places known as repair cafés designated to repairing or mending a variety of items, including clothing and textiles. The advantages of such repair efforts are twofold: If something is fixed—for instance an old sweater—it means not only is that sweater saved from landfill, a new one is not needed.

Designing for repairability means identifying the key features of a garment that may require repair or replacement due to wear and tear. Zippers, zipper pulls, threads, yarns, patches, and buckles can be offered in an easy-to-use repair kit, together with guidance on making the repair.

For the user, extending the life of a product should be a simple task. Outdoor lifestyle brand Imperial Motion sells garments and backpacks made of a lightweight, water-resistant nylon called "Nano Cure Tech" that allows for the self-repair of small holes. When torn, the coated edges can be put together and with the heat of a finger the fabric repairs itself.

Poster issued by the Board of Trade, UK, c. 1944, encourages people to be more thrifty.

EMBRACING VISIBLE MENDING

Tom van Deijnen, "Tom of Holland," is a self-taught textiles practitioner based in Brighton, UK. In 2012 he introduced the Visible Mending Programme to provide mending inspiration, reinforce the art and craftsmanship of clothing repair, and explore stories behind a garment and its wearer. In doing so, he hopes to encourage people to wear their existing clothing for longer. Van Deijnen says: "By exploring the motivations, I favor not the new and perfect but the old and imperfect, that allows me to highlight the relationship between garment and wearer. My interest in using traditional techniques for creating and repairing (woolen) textiles means that creating and mending textiles are in constant conversation with each other." [30]

(tomofholland.com)

BIODEGRABILITY IN DESIGN

Biodegradability is a material's capacity to be broken down by living organisms and decay over time. Designing for biodegradability means selecting materials that decompose naturally and that can be returned to nature after use through a biological cycle. The biodegradability of any fabric is largely determined by the quantity of chemicals used in the material's life cycle. Organic fibers and natural plant dyes are restored to the ecosystem in the most timely and efficient manner.

Fast Fashion retailer C&A, for instance, introduced the world's first Gold-level Cradle to Cradle (C2C) Certified denim jeans. The jeans took more than a year to develop and are made from organic cotton and colored with dye derived from plant waste. C&A is now providing other clothing brands with the tools they need to produce equally sustainable denim garments.

DEMATERIALIZATION IN DESIGN

Dematerialization means reducing or eliminating the amount of materials used in the making of a product. Historically, during wartime, designers were restricted in the amount of materials and trimmings they could use in the production of civilian clothing, as the production of military uniforms took precedent. During World War II in the US, the War Production Board (WPB) issued an order to reduce the amount of textiles used in the production of womenswear clothing. The order prohibited pleats, ruffles, patch pockets, attached hoods and shawls, full skirts, and full sleeves. Skirt lengths and the width of pants (trousers) were also restricted, and even home-sewing patterns followed the WPB guidelines.[31]

Today, designing with dematerialization in mind means valuing materials enough not to waste them. The design intention focuses on reducing waste through resource efficiencies and technological innovations in design techniques and practices.

Resource efficiency means using the Earth's limited resources in a sustainable manner while minimizing impacts on the environment.
European Commission

ZERO-WASTE DESIGN

Zero waste is a design technique that aims to eliminate textile waste at the very beginning of the design process. Some of the simplest designs are inherently zero waste, such as the Japanese kimono. The kimono is traditionally made from a single bolt of fabric called the tanmono. The entire bolt of fabric is used to create four main pieces—two wide body panels, two narrower sleeve panels—and thin strips for the collar.

Zero waste: the conservation of all resources by means of responsible production, consumption, reuse, and recovery of products, packaging, and materials.
Zero Waste International Alliance, zwia.org

Think of zero-waste pattern making as arranging pieces together as you would a jigsaw puzzle to ensure no fabric is wasted during the cutting phase. In 2016, for instance, Miranda Bennett Studio launched the MBS Zero Waste initiative, which collects and organizes leftover fabric cuttings. These remnants then serve as a starting point for new products in accessories, children's clothing, and home goods. Any textiles that cannot be reused are donated to a local quilt guild or charitable cause.

WEARABLE TECHNOLOGY

BioCouture is a community of innovators dedicated to pioneering the use of compostable and biodegradable materials from microorganisms like fungi, algae, bacteria, and cellulose to create clothing. In 2014, designer Suzanne Lee made jackets and shoes from materials produced with bacterial cellulose, a material with similar properties to leather.[32]

Biodegradable, plant-dyed
dresses from Miranda Bennett
Studio, Austin, Texas.

Digital clothing, another facet of wearable technology, merges fashion design and technology, so that garments are designed and exist only virtually. In 2019, the first digital couture outfit was designed by The Fabricant, an Amsterdam-based digital fashion house, and auctioned off for a winning bid of $9,500.[33] The idea behind 3D fashion is that, by allowing consumers to express their sartorial identity digitally on social media, there will be less need for them to buy as many physical garments.

Similarly, the Scandinavian fashion brand Carlings was conceived to make digital fashion more attainable to consumers. All of their collection pieces are solely available as 3D digital models that can be overlaid on any body type. The brand's "digital tailors" manipulate customer photos so it appears as though they are dressed in the apparel, and the garment is then custom fitted. Designing digitally in this way eliminates the need for a physical garment prototype, helping reduce traditional manufacturing, logistics, and transportation supply chain processes and lessening a brand's carbon footprint.

DESIGNING WITH WASTE: UPCYCLING/RECYCLING

Upcycling involves the making of furniture, objects, or garments from old or used items or waste material, creating a product of higher quality than the original or adding value. Recycling is the process of collecting old paper, glass, plastic, and textiles and converting them into reusable material.

Recycle: to collect and treat used objects and materials that are ready to be thrown out in order to produce materials that can be used again.
Cambridge Dictionary

Pre-consumer textile waste is often left on the factory floor when fabric is cut in the production of garments for large companies. This waste can be collected and resold through recycling efforts. With ingenuity, designers can create patterns from the larger cuts of remnant fabric (upcycling),

Zero Waste Daniel poses with surplus scrap fabric, which he transforms into genderless, one-of-a-kind garments.

while the smaller leftover scraps can be cut into long rectangular strips and handwoven into a new artisanal fabric or spun into new yarn to hand knit a garment (recycling). New York-based designer Daniel Silverstein, known as Zero Waste Daniel, combines the skills of zero waste design, upcyling, and recycling to create unique street wear pieces. Silverstein collages together fabrics that other designers or costume departments and factories would normally throw out with patchwork inserts to create T-shirts, sweatshirts, and pants.

Upcycle: reuse discarded objects or material in such a way as to create a product of higher quality or value than the original.
Oxford Dictionary

Brixton-based clothing and textile designer Isabel Fletcher takes inspiration from the overlooked, undervalued fabric scraps and trimmed thread she accumulates from clothing manufacturers. Each made-to-order garment is the result of extensive experimentation, in which she combines techniques such as zero-waste pattern cutting, collage, embroidery, hand sewing, quilting, and appliqué work. La Femme Rousse is a Danish made-to-order circular fashion brand with a similar ethos. Their vision is to eliminate, or at least minimize, the use of pure virgin materials. Designer Susanne Guldager focuses on giving new life to materials that have otherwise served their original purpose. For example, the stains and abrasions of discarded sheets are cut off leaving valuable, usable material. In a time when we are thinking differently about the way we manufacture fashion products, La Femme Rousse produces its

La Femme Rousse's "circular shirt" made from discarded sheets, by Susanne Guldager, Copenhagen.

Modular coat designed for disassembly and versatility by designer Vera de Pont.

Left and right: Thanks to its dissolvable thread, Resortecs®' bomber jacket can be disassembled in five minutes.

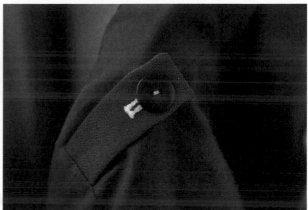

collections locally in collaboration with Sylab, an experimental sewing studio that helps designers reduce their environmental impact through the use of sewing robots and optimal production processes.

DISASSEMBLY IN DESIGN

Design for disassembly takes its cue from sustainable architecture. It is one of the six core principles within the Cradle to Cradle Certified™/Built Positive movement, in which buildings and products are designed intentionally for material recovery, value retention, and meaningful next use. When designing for disassembly, materials, products, and components must be easily separated and then easily reassembled without damage so that they can be recovered, with their value retained, and then meaningfully recycled. There are three important rules for disassembly in design:

1. **Careful selection and use of materials:** If you check the label of a garment you are wearing right now, there is a high chance that the fabric is composed of a blend of different fibers, usually a mix of cotton and polyester. When designing for disassembly, it is recommended to use mono materials—materials that consist of one fiber, as these can be easily recycled.
2. **Healthy and safe design of the components and product:** Toxic dyes, glues, or finishes that may cause negative environmental impact should be avoided.

3. **Simple selection and use of fasteners:** Any hardware, trims, or notions should be easy to remove, so they can be recovered and reused. Currently this often has to be done by hand. To speed up the process, Resortecs®, a Belgian company, created a polyester thread that dissolves when heat is applied with a heat gun.

Dutch prototype designer and researcher Vera de Pont experiments to find ways to prevent material waste. Her project Pop Up Clothing comprises garments that can be cut out from a single piece of fabric and assembled by the user without the need for sewing. In de Pont's Modular Collection, 3D printed button fasteners allow for easy assembly and disassembly by the wearer, giving them the ability to change every element of the garment.

> **THINK PIECE:**
> Consider how a garment can be designed for disassembly. Start by identifying each component (material, buttons, trims, linings, etc.) of the product, and then take into account how each component can be reused or recycled.

CASE STUDY #1: CREATE

FILIPPA K: THE THROW AWAY DRESS

Filippa K was founded in 1993 by Filippa Knutsson and Patrik Kihlborg at their kitchen table in Stockholm, Sweden. Inspired by her own wardrobe needs, Filippa aimed to create a brand that recognized the real lives and challenges of modern women and men by offering clothing based on minimalism, quality, and simplicity. It is now a leading fashion brand in Scandinavia, with an e-commerce site and dozens of branded stores.

Filippa K is committed to the four R's: Reduce, Repair, Reuse, and Recycle, and is gradually transforming the business and its collections so that they can become fully circular by 2030. In 2018, the company tested a "circular fast fashion" design approach by creating 100% bio-based and biodegradable short-lived concept dresses: the "Throw Away Dress" (pictured) can be worn a few times before it is tossed into the household compost bin.

Designing for biodegradability in this way begins by selecting materials that decompose naturally within a reasonable amount of time, enriching the soil. Working with a recycling company to guarantee full recyclability, the Filippa K team decided on a non-woven Tencel™ material. This fabric has numerous benefits, as Jodi Everding, Filippa K's Fabric and Trim Manager, explained in the brand's 2018 Sustainability Report: "the material uses less water and energy, since it is not made like a traditional fabric. It is also biodegradable. But the biggest benefit was showing how a non-woven, industrial type of material could be transformed into a chic and wearable garment."

Designer Emilia Castles had some dress designs in mind, but soon discovered that the traditional method of sketching a design and then cutting and sewing the fabric would not achieve the best result; they must let the fabric dictate the design process. To that end, Emilia used a mangle, a type of clothes press, to give the fabric a silk-like feeling that would make it easier to shape and construct.

To dye the dress, they set up a collaborative pop-up lab with HearteartH Production to develop a process that used natural food waste provided by Swedish fruit and vegetable supplier Grönsakshallen Sorunda and grocer Axfood. Although this alternative approach initially posed a real challenge for the team, it eventually led to a sense of freedom, because they were no longer limited to the effects of traditional chemical washings. The team now felt free to experiment with several application methods and techniques, such as watercoloring, sponges, and feathered brushstrokes. These were dictated by the changes in the Tencel™ material, the "menu" of food waste available, and a certain amount of trial-and-error. A dip-dyeing technique using beet, horseradish root, blackberry, turmeric, and avocado created the best natural ombre effect.

DISCUSSION QUESTIONS

1. What are the advantages and disadvantages of using a non-woven Tencel™ material?
2. In what ways does dyeing with food waste differ from conventional dyeing methods?
3. Do you think single use biodegradable clothing can become the fast fashion of the future?
4. How does designing concept garments help Filippa K create future circular product lines?

The QWSTION team oversees the weaving of Bananatex® fabric, made from abacá fiber.

Part 2
Make

03: MATERIALS

The choice of raw materials can have a significant impact on a fashion brand's social and environmental footprint. Across market segments, it determines up to two-thirds of a brand's water, emissions, energy, and land use.[34] Reducing negative impacts of existing materials, selecting less resource-intensive materials that can be recycled more easily, and investing in developing new fibers all advance the path toward circularity.

GLOBAL RESOURCE USE

The world is on track to exceed 9.7 billion people by 2050 due to the rapid industrialization of developing countries like China, Brazil, and India. It is also forecast that there will be a dramatic rise in the global middle class over the next couple of decades. As a result, we can expect an increased demand for clothes and other goods that define middle-income lifestyles. If we assume that consumption patterns continue at their current rate, we will need three times as many natural resources by the year 2050 compared to those used in the year 2000.

Every product created in the world uses natural resources as its basic component, whether this is air, water, land, natural chemicals, or energy. Natural resources are materials or substances that occur without the intervention of humans. These resources are essential to our survival and to the survival of all other living things. Yet, in order to keep pace with population growth and consumption, unsustainable quantities of these resources are extracted.

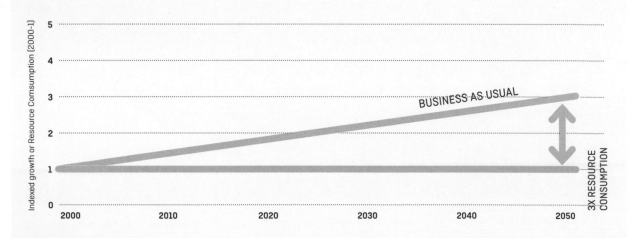

RESOURCE CONSUMPTION SET TO TRIPLE BY 2050

Indexed growth or Resource Consumption (2000-1)

BUSINESS AS USUAL

3X RESOURCE CONSUMPTION

Source: OECD; Fischer-Kowalski et al. 2011

World Footprint: *Today, we require the equivalent of 1.7 Earths to provide the resources we use and to absorb our waste.*
Global Footprint Network, 2019

Resources, such as animals, land, and water, are central to the linear supply chain that has characterized the fashion industry for decades. Vast amounts of natural resources are used up in the industry, which means that if used continuously, they will eventually be depleted. For instance, each year approximately 120 billion cubic yards (92 billion cubic meters) of water is used up by the fashion industry for growing cotton and processing materials—enough water to meet the needs of five million people.[35]

When resources are needed, a circular system selects them wisely and chooses technologies and processes that use renewable sources wherever possible. The fiber and other materials used within a garment account for a significant proportion of its environmental impact. Selecting materials derived from renewable sources and processed using

renewable sources is, therefore, under our control and as such represents a key area where we can shift to more sustainable and circular alternatives.

CIRCULAR CYCLES

Based on the laws of nature, the Cradle to Cradle model recognizes two cycles within which materials flow in a closed loop: the biological cycle and the technical cycle. The technical (industrial) cycle of producing, using, and disposing of materials proposed in the model imitates the biological (natural) cycle of processes of the ecosystem. In the same way that one organism's waste provides nourishment for other living things in the natural world, materials can circulate and provide nutrients for industry.

RENEWABLE RESOURCES ARE CAPABLE OF BEING REPLACED BY ECOLOGICAL PRACTICES OR SOUND MANAGEMENT. *MERRIAM-WEBSTER DICTIONARY*	NON-RENEWABLE RESOURCES ARE UNABLE TO BE REPLACED OR REPLENISHED ONCE USED. *MERRIAM-WEBSTER DICTIONARY*
Fresh Water	Plastics
Solar Energy	Gasoline (Petrol) and Diesel
Biomass	Coal
Oxygen	Natural Gas

BIOLOGICAL CYCLE

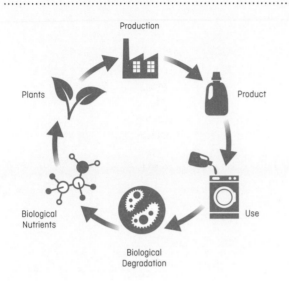

TECHNICAL CYCLE

BIOLOGICAL CYCLES: RESTORATION AND REGENERATION

If designers want to make a good choice straight away, an obvious place to start is by designing with biodegradable and renewable materials that can be used and safely returned to the environment. Biological cycles regenerate living systems, such as soil, which can provide renewable resources for the economy. Materials suitable for a biological cycle are ones that can be returned to the environment during or after their use phase. Generally, the majority of fabrics will eventually biodegrade, whether they are natural or artificial or synthetic fibers. However, the amount of time it takes for a fabric to decompose, along with the amount of environmental damage the process entails, will vary depending largely on the composition of the fiber.

Biodegradable: *able to decay naturally and in a way that is not harmful to the environment.*
Cambridge English Dictionary

Natural materials follow a different and distinct reuse process to synthetic or technical materials. Biological cycles can renew and restore living systems, such as soil, which can provide valuable resources for the economy. Biodegradable materials made from plants, such as cotton, silk, hemp, and linen, and some animals (wool), can be absorbed and thus restored in the ecosystem by means of regeneration. These materials must be free of any toxic chemicals so they are able to decay naturally and properly in the soil. Because of this, it is important to understand when designing materials as a textile designer, or sourcing them for the purpose of fashion design or product development, where the product and its materials will end up after use. Consumption, or the using up of a material, can only occur in biological cycles where the biologically based natural materials are designed to feed back into the system through regenerative and environmentally friendly processes.

Synthetic fabrics are, in theory, able to biodegrade. However, they take far longer to do so and are saturated with a great many chemicals, causing them to emit greenhouse gases, such as methane, into the environment. Typically, the more chemicals used in its fabrication, the longer a fabric takes to biodegrade. To illustrate, a 100% polyester shirt will take up to 20 years to break down in the ecosystem, while some synthetic fibers, such as plastics, may take up to a thousand years!

TECHNICAL CYCLES: RECOVERY AND RESTORATION

Materials suitable for a technical cycle are ones that cannot be consumed or otherwise processed by a biological system. Non-renewable synthetic materials, such as nylon, polyester, plastics, and metals, are also non-biodegradable because they cannot be absorbed back into the ecosystem. However, they can be part of a closed-loop system and circulate in a perpetual cycle of production, recovery, and remanufacture.

> **Non-Biodegradable: *a substance or chemical that is non-biodegradable cannot be changed to a harmless natural state by the action of bacteria, and may therefore damage the environment.***
> Oxford Learner's Dictionary

It is important that these non-biodegradable materials are properly managed so they do not end up in landfills using precious land and releasing harmful gases. Technical cycles exist to recover and restore these materials through strategies like reuse, repair, remanufacture, or recycling.[36]

REUSE
When an item of clothing is reused, it is used again without throwing it away. For example, clothing rental services allow consumers to borrow and wear clothing for a fee.

REPAIR
The garment is returned back to the company to restore or repair and sell again, such as used and vintage clothing. Garment collection programs encourage brands and retailers to take responsibility for the entire life cycle of all their products and encourage consumers to donate their clothing back to the brand after use.

REMANUFACTURE
The discarded clothing, fabric scraps, trimmings, and accessories can be used again in the manufacturing process to create new products.

RECYCLE
The product is recycled to be used in another industry. For example, Nike transforms old, worn-out athletic shoes into Nike Grind, a material used to create courts, tracks, fields, and playgrounds.

REUSE: Subscription rental clothing from LENA Fashion Library.

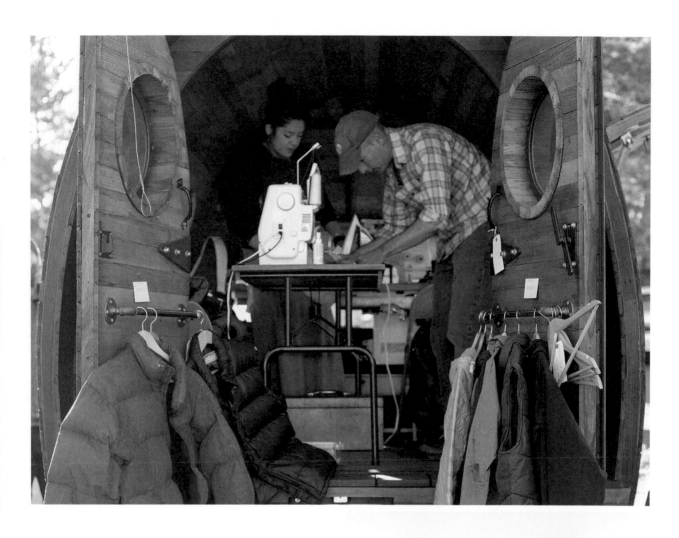

Above: REPAIR: Traveling repair truck from Patagonia.

Right: REMANUFACTURE: Freitag Messenger bag made from used truck tarpaulins, car seat belts, and bicycle inner tubes.

CIRCULARITY AND RESOURCES

Every fiber has advantages and disadvantages. However, as designers increasingly begin designing for circularity, they are discovering alternatives to traditional resources. By selecting biodegradable materials or organic, recycled, or innovative ones, and by understanding the materials cycle with which the designed product is most aligned, designers can reduce resource consumption and decrease negative environmental impacts, such as soil contamination, microfiber shedding, and loss of biodiversity.

ORGANIC FIBERS

Organically grown fibers are the optimal material choice in a biological cycle because they restore and regenerate the soil and protect the health of the wider community. Organic textiles are completely based on fibers grown on organic farms according to strict guidelines. Farmers growing organic fiber follow standards that care for the soil, animals, and people involved in its production and do not use toxic insecticides, herbicides, or fungicides.

There are two independent standards for tracking and verifying the content of organically grown materials. The

Organic Content Standard (OCS) verifies the presence of between 5% to 100% organically grown material in any non-food product by an accredited third party.

The Global Organic Textile Standard (GOTS) covers the whole textile supply chain and requires a minimum of 70% organic content, with requirements covering the remaining non-organic percentage. If a textile is certified as organic by GOTS, it means that both the production of the fiber on the farm and the processing of this fiber into textiles has met organic standards. For instance, organic fiber is bleached using an oxygen-based bleach instead of chlorine, and dyed with low-impact dyes. Every stage of processing is focused on doing the least amount of damage to the environment as possible.

KNOW YOUR FIBERS	
Biodegradable	**Non-biodegradable**
Organic cotton	PVC
Silk	Polyester
Hemp	Spandex
Wool	Nylon
Organic bamboo	Rayon (viscose)
Jute	Conventional cotton
Ramie	Fur
Linen	Leather
Organic fabrications	Chemically treated fabrications
Untreated fabrications	Adhesives, glues, solvents, etc.

The Global Organic Textile Standard certification logo.

RECYCLED YARNS

Recycled yarns are made of pre-consumer waste, the industrial waste from manufacturing garments, meaning all the leftover pieces of fabric from the cutting process (see pages 37–8). The waste is sorted by color and re-spun into yarn. The process significantly reduces environmental impact by reducing the use of virgin material as well as the need for dye processes, thus saving energy and water use.

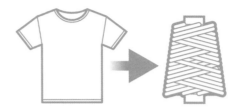

INNOVATIVE MATERIALS

Investment in innovation is a key driver toward circularity in this sector. When it comes to new technologies in sustainable fabrics, the challenges arise in scalability. For instance, how can the substitutes for leather (see pages 63–5) be made easily available?

Circular design leaders need to discover new sustainable raw materials that reduce resource consumption, work with existing material streams, and reduce negative impacts. The environmental and economic rewards have the potential to be substantial, especially considering the increasing scarcity of natural resources and growing population and consumer demand.

NATURAL MATERIALS

Natural materials are sourced directly from nature, be it from animals (such as wool or fur), insects (such as silk), or plants (such as cotton, hemp, or jute). Choosing the correct fibers for a designed product maximizes its longevity and therefore greatly impacts on its circularity.

ANIMAL FIBERS

It is not often we think of animals as fashion products, yet they have been an important part of clothing humans for centuries. Producing fashion apparel and accessories with animal materials often entails the overbreeding and farming of a certain animal, the creation of organic and toxic waste, and the extreme use of resources. However, a number of innovations across many industries mean that there are sustainable alternatives to using animal materials.

FUR

Originally, animals were hunted or trapped for food and their pelts (skins with fur, hair, or wool still on) were used as protective clothing against harsh, cold climates. As society and civilization evolved, furs became less a necessity and more a luxury. Today, the fur trade is a global cold-weather clothing business enterprise.

The pelts of fur-bearing animals consist of two elements: ground hair, a dense undercoat that protects the underlying fur and skin from weather conditions such as rain or snow, and longer hairs known as guard hair that regulate an animal's body temperature.The best quality and color of fur is obtained by trapping animals during the height of winter, when the hair is at its longest, thickest, and shiniest. The finest hair can be found on animals in the Artic and northern regions of the world.

It has been estimated that in recent years more than one billion rabbits and 50 million other animals, including foxes, seals, mink, and raccoon dogs, have been farmed or captured to be killed for their pelts each year. According to PETA (People for the Ethical Treatment of Animals), "the amount of energy needed to produce a real fur coat from ranch-raised animal skins is approximately 15 times that needed to produce a fake fur garment...nor is fur biodegradable due to the chemical treatment applied to stop the fur from rotting."[37]

Fur farming: *the act or process of raising fur-bearing animals commercially for their pelts.*
Merriam-Webster Dictionary

Thankfully in 2018, following a decision made by the British Fashion Council, London Fashion Week became the first of the international fashion weeks to ban animal fur from every one of its fashion shows. Around the same time many luxury fashion brands, such as Prada, Burberry, Gucci, and Michael Kors, pledged to go fur-free, marking a significant animal rights commitment from the top tier of the industry.

Technological advances in fabrics now allow a designer to create a luxe aesthetic using non-animal fur. However, faux furs are not necessarily the best alternative as they are not biodegradable and are typically made from synthetic polymeric fibers, such as acrylic, modacrylic, and/or polyester, all of which are essentially forms of plastic. Faux fur sheds and these small fibers eventually end up in the ocean (see page 136).

Newer animal-free upcyling/recycling innovations include denim fur made from repurposed market jeans, hemp fur from the cannabis plant, and recycled plastic fur (see page 67).

LEATHER

Leather is the most widely used animal skin in fashion products. It is a versatile material known for its high tensile strength, water resistance, and aesthetic surface patterns. The softness of leather is associated with its thickness: thin leathers are generally used for gloves, linings, and clothing; a medium thickness is used for shoes, handbags, and accessories; thicker leathers are used to create the soles of footwear.

The leather industry relies on animals such as cows, buffaloes, deer, and kangaroos. There is also high demand for exotic animal skins in the luxury sector of the fashion industry. Between 2008 and 2017, more than 6.3 million whole skins and more than four million pieces of protected snakes, crocodiles, and lizards were imported by EU (European Union) countries.[38]

Leather can be made of any type of skin or hide. The chemical processes used to give specific properties and functionality to the hides of large animals and the skins of small animals while they are being converted to leather is known as "tanning."

Tanning is done in one of two ways. The oldest and most intricate process is vegetable tanning. Vegetable tanning is an organic method relying on natural vegetable tannins from bark or other plant tissues. In the past two decades, there has been a renewed interest in vegetable tanning due to the natural patina and luxurious touch the process creates.

Chromium tanning, invented in 1858 and adopted during the Industrial Revolution, is a significantly faster method of tanning. It uses a solution of chemicals, acids, and salts to dye the hide. The number of chemical processes applied to raw leather means the material loses all of its natural and sustainable properties. Chromium tanned leather is toxic and does not easily biodegrade.

Artificial leather, also known as pleather, leatherette, or vegan leather, was gradually introduced during the second half of the twentieth century to imitate real leather. However, like faux fur, it is composed of several synthetic fibers. It is created by covering a natural or man-made fabric with polyurethane or polyvinyl chloride (PVC) plastic. PVC is most dangerous, as it releases chemicals (dioxins) which are harmful to humans and animals. Also, synthetic leather does not decompose and damages the soil where it remains indefinitely.

Two men loading raw hides at Barrow Hepburn and Gale Grange Mills, Bermondsey, London [undated].

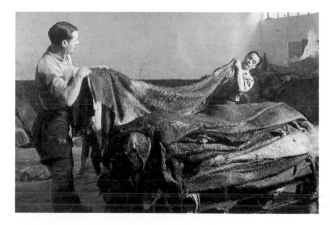

Sustainable leather alternatives are made from cork, pineapple leaves, and mushrooms peels (see pages 63–5), although these are still in the experimental phase with limited production.

Selfridges, the luxury British department store, was one of the first department stores to ban the sale of fur in 2005, although it continues to sell leather goods made from agricultural livestock.[39] A growing number of global retailers and brands, such as Chanel and Victoria Beckham in 2020, have also banned the use of exotic skins, such as snake, alligator, and crocodile, in fashion products such as watches, handbags, and belts. In the United States, California became the first state to ban the sale of products containing exotic animal skins and furs in 2020. California was also the first state to ban the sale of fur.[40]

FEATHERS

Birds such as ostriches, peacocks, doves, geese, and turkeys are some of the species from which feathers are collected. Feathers are generally considered a by-product in much the same way leather is a by-product of the meat industry. The intricate structures on many feathers create a smooth, flexible, and resilient surface, and can be found in a variety of natural colorways.

For thousands of years, feathers have been widely used. The earliest pillows were filled with feathers and down, and writing instruments were made from the quill (hollow shaft) of goose feathers. In the nineteenth century, the focus on the natural world in fashion and in the home sparked an international trend. Stylish women wore hats with the latest feather designs. Milliners in Europe and the US used birds and bird feathers indiscriminately to compete for the most exotic hat designs. As the increase in demand for feathers reached its peak, some wealthier, outlandish women even wore whole bodies of birds as personal adornment.

Throughout the following decades, a growing middle class emulated the fashionable elite. Men wore fedoras with feather trims and women continued to adorn their hats, hair, and clothing with a variety of plumage, particularly ostrich.

Above: A satirical poster called *Woman Behind the Gun*, by Gordon Ross, 1911. The two gundogs are labeled French Milliner.

Below: Women prepare ostrich feathers, France, 1908.

Ostriches are commonly used in the fashion industry because of their lush, luxurious plumage and versatility in that they can be dyed in any color. Ostrich feathers may be acquired in one of two ways: plucking the feathers while the bird is alive or taken from the bird after it has been slaughtered for its skin or meat. Feathers that have been bleached, colored, or dyed with chemical dyes are not biodegradable.

The Responsible Down Standard (RDS) is an independent voluntary global standard that focuses on respect for animal

FEATHERS IN FASHION

The use of feathers in the fashion industry has been controversial for a long time. In 1918, the groundbreaking Migratory Bird Treaty Act, administered by the US Fish and Wildlife Service, prohibited the hunting, killing, trading, and shipping of migratory birds. It also regulated the nation's commercial plume trade, which had decimated many American bird species to the point of near extinction. Prior to the treaty, statistics show that one-and-a-half tons of egret feathers were sold in 1902. According to contemporary estimates, this calculates at 200,000 birds and three times that many eggs. Other figures indicate that the number of birds being killed by hunters in Florida alone each year was as high as five million.[41]

Mary Katrantzou, London Fashion
Week, Fall/Winter 2019.

welfare and the protection of the Five Freedoms: freedom from hunger and thirst, freedom from discomfort, freedom from pain, injury, or disease, freedom to express normal behavior, and freedom from fear and distress. Launched in 2014 by US outerwear brand The North Face in partnership with Textile Exchange (a non-profit organization dedicated to sustainability in the textile industry), RDS aims to ensure that down and feathers come from birds that have not been subjected to unnecessary harm. Each stage in the supply chain is audited by a professional, third party certification body. Only products with 100% certified down and feathers carry the RDS logo.

Closing the loop is feather and down supplier Re:down®. Re:down® recycles down and feathers from post-consumer goods collected all over Europe. The down and feathers are extracted, washed, and sterilized so that they can be re-used in apparel and bedding items.[42]

WOOL

When compared to the leather and fur industries, some people consider wool more ethical, since it does not involve killing animals. Sheep, goats, alpacas, and llamas are sheared to remove their fleece. Although this does make the practice of extracting wool more ethical, lack of regulation means not all companies use wool that derives from farms where the sheep are treated correctly. Overgrazing occurs when a large quantity of livestock, such as sheep and goats, feed too heavily on grass in one area and the land is inadequate to sustain the number of animals. Soil erosion, land degradation, and loss of useful plant species are some of the adverse effects and damages caused by overgrazing.

The Responsible Wool Standard (RWS), introduced in 2016, is a voluntary global standard that addresses the welfare of sheep and the land they graze on (responsiblewool.org). The goals of the RWS are to provide the industry with a tool to recognize the best practices of farmers, ensuring that wool comes from farms with a progressive approach to managing their land and from sheep that have been treated responsibly.

Another consideration when choosing to use wool is the environmental impact of the methane released by the sheep. According to the United Nations' (UN) Food and Agriculture Organization (FAO), livestock are responsible for about 14.5% of global greenhouse gas emissions.

However, wool is the most easily reused of all textile fibers. Recycling wool is a relatively low-impact closed-loop process, which means the wool is deconstructed and the fiber is reused as yarn in new items. Indeed, due to the high quality and durability of the wool fiber, wool products can be circulated for a relatively long period of time, thereby reducing their environmental footprint.

Also, despite its durability, wool is biodegradable. The Campaign for Wool is a global endeavor presided over by its patron His Royal Highness The Prince of Wales, which since 2010 has aimed to educate consumers about the unique, natural, renewable, and biodegradable benefits offered by the fiber. For example, he carried out an experiment in 2016 to establish the comparative qualities of wool and synthetic fiber, burying two jumpers in a flower bed. Approximately six

Opposite and below: Sweaters from
Everlane's ReCashmere range
comprise 60% recycled cashmere
and 40% merino wool.

It takes approximately four goats to produce enough hair
to create one sweater. Producers comb out the hair, sort it by
hand, and send it to be cleaned, refined, baled, and shipped
to textile companies. Historically, the rarity of the fiber made
cashmere a luxurious material only available at a high price
point. The increasing speed-to-market fashion cycle has
increased demand for cashmere and, along with pressure to
lower costs, has resulted in a decrease in price. More goats are
now needed to produce the same amount of cashmere,
resulting in overpopulation and unsustainable toxic land use.

Many fashion brands are now replacing virgin cashmere
with a regenerated variety. Recycled cashmere can be
collected from factory scraps and used garments and spun
into renewed yarns. These yarns can then be used to create
new fashion products. Cashmere recycling programs ask
consumers to send back their old cashmere sweaters for
an incentive. Once a brand has collected a substantial
number of sweaters, they are sent to a mill for processing.

One of the disadvantages of recycled cashmere is that the
yarns are broken down, making them weaker and more
susceptible to pilling and damage. To ensure the quality is
comparable to virgin fiber, some mills are blending recycled
cashmere with extra fine merino wool.

SILK

Silk is known for its unique properties: luster, shine, tensile
strength, durability, and luxurious drape. It is highly
absorbent and has an excellent affinity for dyes. Fabrics
made from silk can keep the wearer cool in the summer
or warmer in the winter.

Silk farming or sericulture is the production of silk using
domestic silkworms. It is a labor-intensive process that
has remained unchanged for centuries and approximately
one million workers are employed in the industry in China.[43]

The silkworm is the larva of a moth and a commercially
bred caterpillar. Each silkworm spins a cocoon and the pupa
is destroyed before it emerges. Cocoons are then cooked
and the silk filament extracted by reeling. Washing silk to
de-gum it and dyeing both require many harsh and intensive

months later, an exhumation revealed an intact synthetic
jumper while the woolen jumper had decomposed into
the soil.

Cashmere

Cashmere is a natural biodegradable fiber made from the
soft, fleecy hair in the underbelly of goats. Although all goats
produce cashmere, the nomadic breed that produces the
finest hairs are found in Mongolia, Southwest China, Tibet,
Iran, Northern India, and Afghanistan.

Cashmere goats have little fat and their coats offer
protection from the harsh winter climates. They naturally
shed their coats as the temperature rises. However, in the
cashmere industry, their coats are shorn during midwinter,
making them vulnerable to frigid temperatures.

Adidas x Stella McCartney
Microsilk™ Tennis Dress by
Bolt Threads.

treatments, including chemicals that can pollute the groundwater. Silk production is very labor-intensive and uses large amounts of resources which yield a small amount of silk. Estimates suggest that only 33 to 40 pounds (15 to 18 kg) of silk come from one acre (0.4 ha) of mulberry trees and approximately 6,600 silkworms are killed to make 2.2 pounds (1 kg) of silk.[44]

Peace Silk

Ahisma or Peace Silk is marketed as a cruelty-free, ethical alternative to silk because it allows for the natural completion of the metamorphosis of the silkworm to the moth. The silkworms grow in trees without the use of fungicides, insecticides, or genetic sprays. For protection from birds and other insects a net is placed over the entire tree. Once the cocoons have been spun, they are sheltered until the pupae hatch out, which generally takes two to four weeks. Once the moths leave the cocoons, the empty cocoons are processed without the use of toxic chemicals.

Non-violent silk breeding and harvesting slows silk production and its costs are higher than traditional silk processes. Animal rights group PETA warns of poor social and animal rights practices associated with its production methods. Additionally, no certification exists yet to authenticate or uphold these non-conventional standards.[45]

Synthetic spider vegan silk

Spiders produce natural silk fibers with performance properties such as high tensile strength, softness, durability, and elasticity.

To create Microsilk™, California start-up Bolt Threads studied the characteristics of the silk proteins spun by spiders. Inspired by the silk, they developed proteins by using bioengineering to put genes into yeast. These proteins are then produced in large quantities through fermentation using yeast, sugar, and water. Liquid silk proteins are then extracted and spun into yarns to weave for apparel.

Although still in the research and development phase, Microsilk™ has the potential to create a completely closed circular loop. Adidas and fashion designer Stella McCartney used Microsilk™ to introduce a biofabric tennis dress. The vegan silk was blended with a cellulosic fiber, an organic compound found in plant cells, which eventually breaks back down into the environment, making the tennis dress fully biodegradable at the end of its life.

PLANT FIBERS

Plant fibers are generally composed of cellulose—the main constituent of plant cell walls. Cellulosic fiber can be found in a plant's leaves, stems or stalks, seed pods, or fruit. Plant fibers are classified as follows:

Bast or stem fibers, derived from the fibrous bundles in the inner bark of plant stems (flax or hemp).

Leaf fibers, which run lengthwise through the leaves of plants (pineapples, raffia palms).

Seed-hair fibers (cotton).

LINEN

Linen is derived from the stem of the flax plant, a natural raw material. Linen is one of the world's oldest textiles, known to have been used in the Stone Age, and it is a recyclable fiber. All parts of the plant are used, ensuring minimal waste.

Historically, flax has grown best in the rich soils and climate of northern France, Belgium, and the Netherlands, where 80% of the world's flax is still produced. Compared to cotton, flax requires very little water because the plant can thrive solely on rainwater and without irrigation methods.

Linen fibers are durable and strong; twice as strong as cotton ones. The fabric is lightweight and becomes softer and more lustrous with use and laundering, allowing it to be worn for a long time. Heirloom linens handed down through generations may show these qualities. Linen is regarded as a "cool" fabric, as it absorbs moisture quickly, making it comfortable and ideal to wear in warm climates. Although possessing natural textural properties, most linen is treated, bleached, or dyed.

Organic linen is untreated, meaning no chemicals are used during production, thereby ensuring it is completely biodegradable and restorative to the soil. Organic textile production certification, such as GOTS, is designed to ensure ecological and social criteria are met and also limits the use of chemicals, such as toxins, bleaches, or dyes, during processing. Although organic linen products are more expensive, investment in organic fibers by producers and consumers promotes overall long-term health for farmers, the environment, and communities.

Organic linen by Komodo.

Since 2013, Eileen Fisher has been sourcing its linen from a 2,000-acre (810-ha) organic farm in western China. The company also uses mills there for spinning, producing more than half a million organic linen garments a year.[46]

LINEN PRODUCTION

1 Cultivation → 2 Flowering → 3 Pulling → 4 Retting → 5 Harvest → 6 Scutching → 7 Combing → 8 Spinning → 9 Knitting or weaving

Left: The Vintage Crew by closed-loop clothing brand For Days, made from 50% upcycled cotton and 50% organic cotton.

Above right: A stylish knit made from 100% organic cotton by H&M.

Bottom right: Spinning yarn as cotton is recycled at Textil Santanderina, Spain, using state-of-the-art textile machinery.

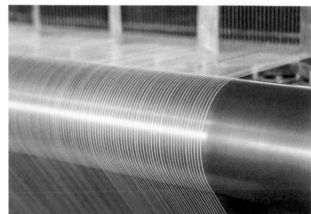

COTTON

Approximately half of all textiles produced today are made of cotton. It is the most widely used fiber in the apparel industry because of its qualities of comfort and natural absorbency. Today, cotton production employs more than 250 million people worldwide, mostly in developing countries such as India and Bangladesh, where labor costs are cheaper.[47]

A natural fiber which comes from the seedpod of the cotton plant, cotton is easy to clean, but is prone to shrinkage, so it may be blended with synthetic fibers and treated with chemical finishes to enhance its properties. Cotton fiber can be knitted or woven into fabric.

Conventional cotton is the most resource-intensive crop produced in the world. It is grown from genetically modified seeds (GMOs) and relies on the heavy use of water, synthetic agrochemicals, and large areas of land that maximize crop yields at the expense of the soil. Harmful agrochemicals used by farmers, including fertilizers, insecticides, and herbicides, can seep into waterways and pollute the surrounding environment, affecting communities and the wider ecosystem.

Organic cotton, on the other hand, is grown without chemicals and genetically modified seeds. Organic cotton farmers can collect and replant cotton seeds. Although more expensive

RECYCLING COTTON

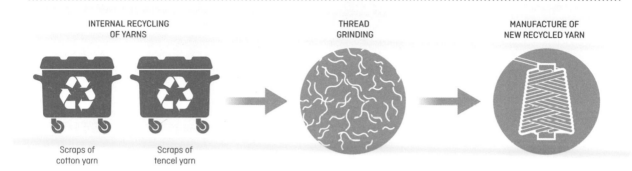

INTERNAL RECYCLING
OF YARNS

Scraps of
cotton yarn

Scraps of
tencel yarn

THREAD
GRINDING

MANUFACTURE OF
NEW RECYCLED YARN

than conventional cotton, benefits include a reduction in water because most of the organic cotton is rain fed, and a reduction in both carbon emissions and toxic waste.

The Better Cotton Initiative (BCI) is a global non-profit organization dedicated to promoting better global cotton farming production practices. BCI farmers produced more than five million metric tons of "Better Cotton"—that accounts for around 19% of global cotton production.[48] Australian retailer Cotton On sources sustainable cotton through a partnership with the Better Cotton Initiative.

Recycled cotton

Recycled cotton involves converting cotton fabric into cotton fiber that can be reused in textile products. The largest volume of recycled cotton is produced through pre-consumer waste, such as cutting scraps.

Recycled cotton often provides a good alternative to non-circular fabrics. For example, designer Tiziano Guardini experimented with several alternatives to create vegan fur, including pine needles, before he partnered with denim supplier ISKO to co-create denim fur. The result, made with both organic and pre-consumer recycled cotton, provides a sustainable alternative to both animal and synthetic fur. Similarly, Ksenia Schnaider, a small Ukrainian brand, shops

the secondhand markets in Kiev for used denim jeans to repurpose into luxury fashion sportswear, including their innovative denim fur coat.

HEMP

Industrial hemp can be grown as a renewable source for raw materials for apparel and accessories. It grows without chemicals in any climate, with minimal water use. Cultivation of the plant can restore the health of the soil.

Two kinds of fibers are derived from the hemp plant's stalk. These are long (bast) fibers and short (core) fibers. Bast fibers can be cleaned, spun, and then woven or knitted into many fabrics suitable for durability in design. Hemp fibers can be blended with other fibers, such as cotton and linen, for specific textures and performance.

Hemp is lightweight, warm, and hypoallergenic, and has weather-resistant properties. It provides many advantages over other textiles. It is much stronger and more durable than cotton and also 100% biodegradable. Overall, it has a much smaller environmental footprint than conventionally grown cotton.

Hemp is another fiber that has been used to produce a sustainable alternative to fur. Amsterdam-based Hoodlamb

COMPOSTABLE CLOTHES

Zurich-based clothing manufacturer Freitag is producing apparel made from material that is specifically designed for biodegradability. The material, known as F-abric, is made from a blend of flax and hemp fibers, along with modal fibers made by spinning cellulose obtained from beech trees. A special weaving process contributes to the textile's ability to readily disintegrate once composted.

CIRCULAR LEADERS: DANIEL FREITAG AND MARKUS FREITAG

In 1993, brothers Daniel and Markus Freitag were two Swiss college students and keen commuter cyclists in need of a functional travel bag for biking in unpredictable weather. Inspiration finally came from the trucks that passed by their flat: Their first durable and waterproof bag was made from recycled truck tarpaulin, along with old bicycle inner tubes and car seat belts. Today, this messenger bag is a bestseller and can be found strapped on fellow urban bikers in cities all over the world.

To make their bags, Freitag collects the truck tarps, takes them apart, then washes and cuts them to size, with each bag reflecting the unique colors, markings, and contours of the tarpaulin from which it is made. The brand's product line now comprises 90 models of the messenger bag, and a variety of laptop bags, backpacks, and other bike-able accessories.

The Freitag philosophy is based on thinking and acting in cycles. Since 2015, the company has practiced holacracy, a self-management structure where decision making is distributed across the company in the form of circles (teams), rather than the traditional linear structure of supervisors and managers.

(freitag.ch)

designs winter outerwear using a cruelty-free hemp fur known as Satifur, made of recycled (PET) bottles and hemp. Also, Ukrainian brand DevoHome manufactures all its clothing and home products from hemp fibers. The cultivation and harvesting are performed in the fields near its factory, where the hemp fiber is processed.

ALTERNATIVE PLANT FIBERS

Sustainable textile innovation is happening at a rapid pace. New fabrics entering the market are more readily available for designers shifting toward circular and sustainable collections. Below are some of the more ecological plant alternatives to replace existing options.

Cork—leather alternative

Cork is made from bark stripped once every decade from oak trees primarily found in Spain, Portugal, and France. The tree can be stripped of the bark with very little processing and without causing any environmental damage. Cork is both recyclable and biodegradable.

Pineapples—leather alternative

Piñatex® is a non-woven material made from the waste parts of a pineapple plant. The fibers are extracted from the leaves and the biomass that remains is composted. The fibers, approximately 480 leaves per yard (meter) of material, are felted into a leather alternative for clothing and accessories. Tooche, a women-owned ethical shoe brand, works with shoemakers in Latvia to handcraft shoes using eco-friendly materials such as wool felt and Piñatex®.

Oranges—silk alternative

Orange Fiber is an Italian company that has patented and manufactures a biodegradable silk alternative repurposed from citrus peels. Following a partnership with Politecnico di Milano University, the innovative process turns more than 700,000 tons of discarded citrus waste produced by the industry in Italy each year into a soft, silky, and lightweight material. In 2015, the company won the H&M Foundation Global Change Award. As a way of highlighting stylish designs with minimal environmental impact, H&M's Conscious Exclusive collection featured clothing from Orange Fiber and Piñatex® in 2019.

Upper: Traditional folkloric fabric and cork handbag from Lisbon, Portugal.

Center: Samples of Piñatex®, an innovative alternative to leather made from pineapple leaf fibers.

Lower: A bandeau from the Ferragamo Orange Fiber Collection S/S 2017, to celebrate Earth Day.

A range of Bananatex® bags
by Swiss brand QWSTION in
development.

Abacá—synthetic alternative

Abacá is a leaf fiber extracted from the sheath-like leaves of
the abacá plant (a species of banana) cultivated in the
highlands of the Philippines. It can be interplanted with other
plants, minimizing soil erosion and requiring less land for its
production. Abacá also helps with the restoration of the
ecosystem and recovery of threatened species.

Abacá fiber is known for its luster, durability, flexibility, and
resistance to saltwater. During the nineteenth century, it was
widely used for making ropes, twines, fishing lines, and nets,
while the pulp was used for sturdy manila envelopes. The
fiber requires no spinning and has strong lightweight inner
fibers primarily used in fashion accessories such as hats
and handbags.

Bananatex® is the first technical waterproof fabric made
from abacá fiber. It is strong and durable, yet lightweight and
flexible, and offers a viable alternative to synthetic fabrics.
The Bananatex® bag collection from Swiss brand QWSTION
is designed to leave zero waste after cutting the individual
parts. At the end of a bag's life cycle the fabric is 100%
biodegradable, and its buckles and zippers can be recycled.

Mushrooms—leather alternative

Mushroom leather is made from mycelium, the root
structure of mushrooms which grows as a wide thread under
the forest floor. Mycelium is a tissue-like structure that
can be made to form a variety of shapes, sizes, and widths
by altering its environmental conditions. For example, if

Bolt Thread's Mylo™ Driver Bag
looks like leather, but it was
created with mylo, a sustainable
material made from mycelium.

placed in a bowl it will take the shape of the bowl. Growing mycelium yields minimal, mostly compostable waste, and uses limited space and energy.

Mycelium is strong, flexible, and durable; its strength coming from adapting to the extreme underground conditions. Similar to leather, it is waterproof, but softer and more breathable.

Bamboo—cotton alternative

Monocel® was developed by Norwegian firm Nankatan as a sustainable alternative to conventional cotton. It is created using third-generation bamboo fiber grown under the Forest Stewardship Council (FSC) standards that support responsible global forestry management. Bamboo plants do not require

any irrigation, pesticides, or fertilizers, and do not suppress food production because they thrive in barren soil conditions not suitable for cultivating food crops.

During the manufacturing process, the bamboo is processed in an an energy- and water-efficient closed-loop system to recycle the non-toxic chemicals, like the process used by Lenzing to produce TENCEL™ (see page 66).

Monocel® yarns are softer—providing a luxurious hand (feel)—and stronger than cotton, when both wet and dry. They are also anti-static and antibacterial, with temperature regulating properties.

ARTIFICIAL AND SYNTHETIC FIBERS

Unnatural fibers are known as artificial or synthetic. Artificial fibers are regenerated by humans from natural sources such as plant cellulose. Synthetic fibers are made of manufactured materials formed through chemical processes.

ARTIFICIAL FIBERS

Cellulosic fibers are a class of materials derived from cellulose, the fibrous substance that makes up a plant's cell walls, extracted from bark, wood, or leaves. Cotton, linen, and hemp are natural fibers from cellulose, while rayon is an artificial cellulosic fiber because it has been broken down to a liquid using chemicals before being shaped into a filament to be spun into thread.

RAYON (VISCOSE)

Rayon (viscose) is the most common form of artificial cellulose. Developed in France in the mid-nineteeth century, the fabric was first marketed as "artificial silk." Today, most production takes place in China. Global production of cellulosic fibers has doubled over the last 20 years, primarily due to the growth of rayon.

Rayon is a versatile fabric with many of the same properties as cotton and silk. It is soft, comfortable, breathable, and absorbent, and takes dyes easily. Rayon drapes well but is prone to wrinkles. Often, rayon is given a chemical wrinkle-resistant finish or is blended with other fibers for better performance properties.

Conventional rayon, also known as viscose, is made from wood pulp from eucalyptus, oak, or birch trees. To transform the wood pulp into a fiber, the pulp is first dissolved using caustic soda (sodium hydroxide), a very corrosive inorganic compound, before it undergoes a series of energy-, water-, and chemically-intensive manufacturing process steps leaving a large carbon footprint.

More sustainable cellulosic processes are available that minimize environmental impact and are designated as "preferred fibers" according to a report by the non-profit organization Textile Exchange, which tracks production of fiber and materials.[49] Rayon, lyocell, and modal are all derived from plant materials, but the difference lies in the manufacturing process and the filament structure.

Lyocell and Modal

Lyocell is a form of rayon developed in 1972 in the US. It is created using a different solvent to conventional rayon to break down the wood pulp. Caustic soda is replaced by a non-toxic organic compound known as N-methylmorpholine N-oxide (NMMO). In a closed-loop production process, the organic solvent is continually reused and recycled with minimal environmental impact.

Lyocell shares many of the properties of rayon, yet it is resistant to wrinkles. It has a smooth, soft surface, with excellent drapeability. It is also durable, breathable, and absorbent. Lyocell is biodegradable, but it costs more to produce and is more expensive than conventional rayon.

TENCEL™ is a brand name for lyocell produced by Austrian supplier Lenzing. TENCEL™ is created using the same production process, but the cellulose fiber is created with wood pulp primarily from eucalyptus trees grown in sustainably harvested forests.

Modal is a form of rayon using the same conventional production process with similar chemicals, but the fibers are treated and stretched to strengthen their filaments. Fabrics made from modal are resistant to shrinkage and piling. Modal was originally developed in Japan in the 1950s, but is now mostly produced by Lenzing.

SYNTHETIC FIBERS

Synthetic fibers are strong, durable, and easy to dye, and provide excellent stain- and water-resistant properties. Cheaper and more easily mass-produced than natural fibers, synthetics are a popular choice for fast fashion brands.

POLYESTER

Polyester, produced from petroleum, is one of the most commonly used fibers in fashion due to its outstanding properties: It is durable, wrinkle and shrinkage resistant, and dries quickly. However, producing polyester carries a very large carbon footprint. According to estimates, 262% more CO_2 is emitted to produce a single polyester T-shirt than a cotton shirt. But substituting polyester with recycled polyester offers up to a 90% reduction of toxic substances, a 60% reduction in energy usage, and up to a 40% dip in emissions, according to the Pulse of the Fashion Industry report 2018.[50]

Recycled polyester is commonly produced from plastic drink bottles (PET bottles). These bottles are melted down and re-spun through a range of processes to create a new polyester material.

PET (polyethylene terephthalate) is a popular polyester, used to produce plastic packaging, textile fibers, and plastic bottles. A French "green chemistry" company, Carbios, has invented a process known as biorecycling that can infinitely recycle PET plastics using enzymes without using a sorting process.

Ocean Plastic
An estimated eight million metric tons of plastic trash ends up in the ocean every year. The ocean currents have formed five gigantic gyres, slow moving whirlpools, where the plastic collects. At current rates, plastic is expected to outweigh all the fish in the sea by 2050.[51]

Artisanal faux fur manufacturer ECOPEL launched a range of faux fur materials created from recycled ocean plastic. The fur is certified by the Global Recycled Standard (GRS). GRS is an international voluntary standard that establishes third-party certification criteria for recycled content, chain of custody, social and environmental practices, and chemical composition restrictions (ecopel.com).

Adidas have teamed up with Parley for the Oceans, a non-profit environmental organization, to tackle the problem of plastic in the ocean. The Adidas x Parley range produces sneakers (trainers) made entirely of yarn recycled from ocean waste, plastic bottles, and illegal deep-sea gill nets.[52]

NYLON
Nylon is another synthetic fiber derived from petroleum. It was developed for DuPont in 1934 as a substitute for silk by American chemist Wallace Carothers. His understanding of polymer molecules, like those in silk, helped with the invention. The fiber is produced using a chemical process called polymerizing, which fuses molecules together to create longer chains.

In comparison to polyester, nylon is more difficult to recycle. Used nylon clothes cannot yet be recycled because their level of contamination is too high due to the blending of

RECYCLING POLYESTER

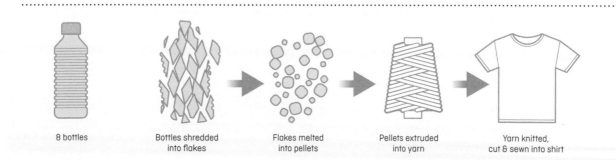

8 bottles   Bottles shredded into flakes   Flakes melted into pellets   Pellets extruded into yarn   Yarn knitted, cut & sewn into shirt

Adidas x Parley's UltraBOOST Parley
sneakers are produced with yarn
recycled from ocean plastic.

fibers and the finishing chemicals added to fabrics.
However, some forms of used nylon can be recycled
using a chemical process to produce suitable recycled
nylon for clothing.

Recycled nylon is principally made from post-industrial
waste (for example, from the virgin nylon yarn production
process or from carpet scraps), but also from post-
consumer waste (used carpets, discarded fishing nets).
This open-loop chemical recycling allows for supply chain
waste reduction, for lower dependence on non-renewable
petroleum resources, and, with post-consumer nylon
waste, for pollution minimization.

BIOWASTE MATERIALS

New bio-based textile developments are shifting toward
circularity by converting waste and by-products from the

food and farming industries into desirable materials for
fashion apparel and accessories. The approach eliminates
the need to cultivate crops for raw materials, while utilizing
existing residue and waste.

BIOPLASTIC

Unlike conventional plastics that are made from petroleum,
bioplastic is a biodegradable plastic made or derived from
renewable natural materials, such as potato, sugar beet, or
cornstarch waste.

A major benefit of bioplastics is their potential to close the
cycle through resource efficiency. The resources used to
create bioplastics can be reused or mechanically recycled
at the end of a product's life cycle, creating rich organic
materials that can be used to grow new plants in the soil.
Chip[s] Board®, a circular materials company founded on the
mission of "finding value where others see waste," make a

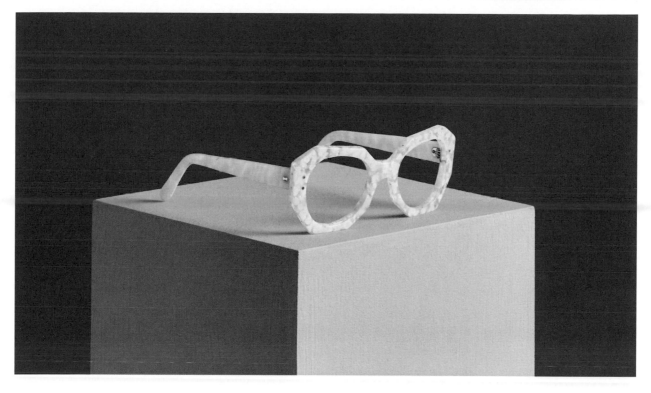

Spectacle frames from Cubitts'
Redux collection. The frames are
made from Parblex®, a potato
biowaste material.

range of materials from potato waste.[53] Partnering with
McCain Foods, and using a zero-waste production system
where peels are regenerated back into the process, potato
peelings are mixed with agricultural waste to create the
company's bioplastic Parblex®. Parblex® has excellent
surface texture and is designed to replace conventional
plastic. It is competitively priced and recommended for
fastenings, buttons, and fashion accessories.

AGRALOOP™ BIOFIBRE

Circular Systems SPC (Social Purpose Company), based in
Los Angeles, won the 2018 H&M Foundation Global Change
award. The materials science start-up converts crop residue
from the farming of hemp, flax, pineapples, bananas, and
sugar cane into a high value textile known as Agraloop™
BioFibre. Without turning farm waste into new materials,
scraps would be left to rot or incinerated, producing
enormous amounts of methane and creating increased

levels of greenhouse gas emissions. New brand partnerships
to create fashion products have been signed with Veja Shoes
and Levi's® among others.

THINK PIECE:
For our circular future, which fabrics do
you believe are the most promising alternatives
for conventional cotton, synthetic polyester, and
animal-derived materials?

CHAPTER 4: PROCESSING

How do we measure the impact on the environment of producing an item of clothing? The type and severity of any impact depends significantly on the material used, and not least on how that material has been processed. Cotton, rayon, polyester, blended fabrics, and recycled fibers are treated in very different ways and require different solutions to mitigate their effect. Chemical use, water use, land use, and the treatment of wastewater are all important considerations.

CHEMICAL USE

Approximately 8,000 synthetic chemicals are used in the processing of raw materials into fashion products, along with over 10,000 different types of dyestuffs.[54] Many of these chemicals contain known carcinogens, chemicals that cause cancer, a fact generally hidden from consumers. These harsh chemicals also pose health hazards to the people who work with them and end up in freshwater systems that surround the factories.

Despite these concerns, fashion retailers are not required to disclose any of the production methods or chemicals that are used in the manufacturing of their products. In the United States, clothing labels only have to disclose the fiber content, where the clothing was created (known as the country of origin), the name of the manufacturer, and care instructions. In the UK, the mandatory requirement for clothing labels are fiber content, country of origin, care instructions, and the flammability of the garment, if applicable.

Both synthetic and natural fabrics can be bleached, dyed, and soaked in chemical baths before being rinsed, a highly water-intensive process. While most chemicals are rinsed off during manufacturing, some may linger on the garments, affecting those handling the product at various points along the supply chain. Clothes that are designed to be wrinkle-free, stain resistant, or UV protected can be treated with finishing chemicals that are inherently built into the fabric.

The majority of textiles are processed in developing countries. Since there is little transparency about the chemicals used in the manufacturing process, workers may be directly exposed to chemicals without adequate safety protection.

POLYFLUORINATED CHEMICALS (PFCS)

PFCs are predominantly used as stain and water repellents for wet-weather garments. PFCs do not break down once they enter the natural environment or a human body, so can damage ecosystems and affect human health, disrupting liver and hormonal functions.[55] In 2014 Greenpeace found

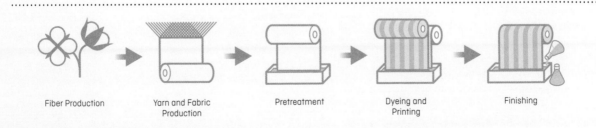

TEXTILE PROCESSING STEPS

Fiber Production → Yarn and Fabric Production → Pretreatment → Dyeing and Printing → Finishing

PFCs in the wastewater of textile factories and in wild fish caught for consumption in China.[56]

FORMALDEHYDE

Formaldehyde is a colorless gas used to make clothing wrinkle- and shrink-resistant, even after multiple washings. This means formaldehyde cannot be rinsed off with detergent and water. The chemical is also used to prevent mildew from forming when clothing is being transported. Formaldehyde is known as a respiratory irritant and has been declared a carcinogen by the International Agency for Research on Cancer.

FLAME RETARDANTS

Flame retardants are used to prevent the spread of fire and are predominantly used for children's pajamas. In the United States, children's pajamas must be flame resistant (or fit snugly), as regulated by the Flammable Fabrics Act of 1953. The chemicals used in these retardants can interfere with hormonal function and may even cause cancer. Children may be particularly vulnerable to the toxic effects of these chemicals because their organs are still developing.

CADMIUM, MERCURY, AND LEAD

Cadmium, mercury, and lead are referred to as "heavy metals." In the fashion industry they are commonly found in dyes and are also used in leather tanning. The toxicity of these metals can accumulate in human cells, causing damage to the nervous system or kidneys.

AZO DYES

Azo dyes make up 60–70% of dyes used in textile manufacturing because they are inexpensive and adhere well to a variety of fibers, producing bright, vibrant colors.[57] Azo dyes also release aromatic amines, known carcinogens.

CHEMICALS AND FIBER PRODUCTION

Natural and man-made fibers all require processing to turn them into material, which means that natural and synthetic fibers alike can have significant environmental impacts. If not grown organically, the cultivation of cotton is enormously resource-intensive, with high inputs of pesticides, insecticides, and fertilizers leaving a large toxic footprint. Pesticides and insecticides are also used to prevent disease in sheep and wool fibers are treated with chemicals during the scouring and washing process.

The production of man-made fibers, such as rayon or lyocell, is also very resource-intensive, involving the use of several hazardous substances before the new fiber is spun. The solvent used in the rayon process, called carbon disulfide, is a toxic chemical that is known to affect the human reproductive system and poses danger to factory workers, surrounding communities, and the environment through air emissions and wastewater.

Polyester fibers rely on non-renewable resources (oil) for fiber production and are also manufactured from many toxic chemicals, such as dihydric acid and terephthalic acid. Both chemicals are not completely removed during the processing stages, resulting in absorption through wet skin which can cause dermatitis and respiratory infections among factory workers. In addition, man-made materials are non-biodegradable and take a long time to decompose, creating long-term pollution.

Given these environmental and human health impacts, the use of chemicals in fiber processing poses a serious challenge. However, as we reimagine a circular approach to fabrics and other materials used in fashion, two key areas of opportunity emerge:

1. Phasing out or eliminating harmful substances that are currently used in manufacturing fiber, apparel, and footwear, and replacing these substances with safer alternatives.
2. Designing materials and products using inherently safer, greener chemistry methods and techniques.

YARN AND FABRIC PRODUCTION

The core of textile manufacturing is fabric production. Fabrics can be created in many ways, the most common being weaving, followed by knitting and then other forms of construction (crochet, felting, etc.). To prevent the yarn from breaking during these processes, several chemical lubricants, solvents, and adhesives are used at various stages to strengthen the yarn or decrease friction.

A denim detail from Versace's Fall/ Winter 2020 presentation at Milan Fashion Week.

Pre-treatment

Pre-treatment processes can be carried out with fibers, yarns, or fabrics before they are subject to wet processing techniques. Pre-treatment prepares the material to accept dyes and additional chemicals, enabling subsequent processing. This is done in a multi-step process and depends on the type or blend of fiber and how it will be treated afterwards.

Dyeing and printing

Dyes used for dyeing material can also be used for printing material, but must undergo the same fixation and washing steps (see page 70). Many dyes present health risks, such as skin diseases, to those working with them, as well as entering into freshwater systems. The dyeing process generally involves a range of toxic chemicals, such as dioxins, that are carcinogenic and may also disrupt hormones. These chemicals include toxic heavy metals, such as chrome, copper, and zinc, that are known carcinogens (capable of causing cancer), and formaldehyde. Other dyes or dye processes include heavy metals like copper, chromium, or cobalt.

Finishing

The final step in textile processing is adding numerous technical properties or an aesthetic appeal to the finished fabric. Depending on the properties desired, such as flame retardancy, enhanced water resistance, antibacterial action, a protective coating, or specific fashion treatment, a diverse range of chemicals are used.

A striking example of how finishing can be damaging is provided by the denim industry. Denim jeans are one of the most ubiquitous items of clothing on this planet with millions of pairs sold worldwide. The global denim jeans market has been forecasted to be worth around $85.4 billion (£65.7 million) in retail sales by 2025.[58] The jeans market has benefitted from numerous innovations such as the fabric being stone-washed, distressed, acid washed, embroidered, studded, and ripped. Bleached denim regularly reappears as a trend on designer runways and is sold in numerous fashion outlets.

Turkey is one of the biggest denim manufacturers in the world. In March 2009, the country banned sandblasting, a technique used to bleach denim, after many workers inhaled the airborne particles and the silica inside caused them to suffer from the terminal lung disease silicosis. Potassium permanganate is now used as a replacement to the sandblasting technique in 90% of the bleaching processes designed to create the look of faded denim. It is an effective finishing technique, but it too presents high risks for the environment and human health. The chemical is classified as "dangerous" by the European Chemical Agency and may affect the lungs if inhaled repeatedly, resulting in symptoms like bronchitis and pneumonia. The chemical contains manganese, which is a heavy metal and not biodegradable.

Worldwide more than five tons of potassium permanganate are used every day, which means an enormous discharge into the wastewaters, causing toxicity in aquatic life. In 2018, the German chemical company CHT Group launched the first ecological alternative to potassium permanganate. "organIQ BLEACH" is an innovative and organic bleaching agent that is free from heavy metals and chlorine, and is completely biodegradable.

Digital finishing

Engraving and etching finishes with a laser machine are a sustainable alternative to the chemical and hand-distressing of denim. Laser technology can emulate naturally faded jeans. In 2019 Levi's® launched Future Finish, the first online customization platform that offers consumers personalization through the use of laser finishing with over 3,000 possible permutations.

GREEN CHEMISTRY

Green chemistry, also known as sustainable chemistry, aims to minimize or eliminate the use of hazardous substances by finding safer more ecological alternatives. It applies across the life cycle of a chemical product, including its design, manufacture, use, and ultimate disposal. Developed by chemists Paul Anastas and John Warner, The 12 Principles of Green Chemistry serve as a blueprint to abolish chemical pollution at its source by encouraging chemists across all disciplines to design less hazardous chemicals

that are not toxic for humans or the environment and that generate no waste. Once used, these chemicals should break down into harmless substances that do not accumulate in waterways, etc.[59] These principles can and should be applied across the fashion industry, particularly in relation to current dyeing practices which, as we have seen, rely heavily on harmful chemicals.

GREENER DYEING PROCESSES

A closer look at new and experimental dyeing techniques provides an encouraging snapshot of the ways in which companies can develop new manufacturing techniques that are less harmful for workers, wearers, and the environment:

Color dyes from bacteria

Color derived from bacteria is a 100% natural biological product. Vienna Textile Lab, for example, fabricates organic colors made by naturally occurring bacteria in order to provide a sustainable and environmentally friendly alternative to conventional synthetic colors.

Crab shell fixative

Luigi Caccia, Founder of PureDenim, had been making denim in northern Italy for more than 40 years when he realized workers were becoming sick and rivers were dying from all the chemicals they were exposed to during production. In 2014, he decided to create a cleaner dyeing process, so his company invested in a machine that uses electrochemicals (CO_2 and O_2) and no water to dye their denim jeans.

Subsequently, the company replaced the traditional technique of processing yarn with polyvinyl alcohol (PVA) to make denim because PVA uses large quantities of water and energy and requires cleaning chemicals that have a considerable negative impact on the quality of wastewater. PVA is a microplastic often found in wastewater, even after intensive purification steps, and is likely to enter the aquatic food chain.

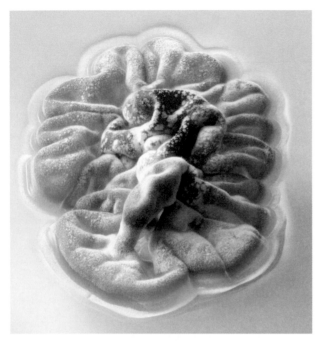

Left: Colony of Streptomyces coelicolor bacteria, which, under the right conditions, becomes pigmented and can be used to dye fabric.

Below: DyeCoo waterless and chemical-free industrial machines provide clean textile processing.

Caccia discovered a company using chitosan (a natural derivative of chitin—the exoskeleton of crustaceans) and applied it to the denim yarn after dyeing it. Chitosan creates a shell to protect the color dyes so they will not rub off, resulting in a reduction in the amount of dye required to color the fabric. Chitosan is also biodegradable, and using it drastically reduces the consumption of water and energy, and the use of toxic detergents, bleach, and other chemical agents.

Waterless dyes

Waterless dyes are another means by which companies can reduce or eliminate the use of water and chemicals in the production process. DyeCoo is a Netherlands-based business that uses a machine to dye fabrics with pressurized CO_2. This allows the dyes to dissolve quickly and penetrate the textile without using chemicals or water. Each machine is estimated to save up to 8.4 million gallons (31.8 million liters) of water and roughly 176 tons of processing chemicals every year. Additionally, since the machine uses a closed-loop system, 95% of the CO_2 can be cleaned and recycled after each dye cycle.[60]

WATER USE

Everything you are wearing today required thousands of pints (liters) of water to produce. Water is a critical component to all manufacturing processes. A water footprint is the volume of water used to create the clothing we wear and consume. By measuring a water footprint, we can get a clear indication of how water is being used.

Water used in global textile production (including cotton farming) adds up to about 24.56 trillion gallons (92.95 trillion liters) each year.[61] The majority of fabric treatment processes, including sizing, scouring, bleaching, mercerizing, and dyeing, use water. And in every one of these steps, a thorough rinsing of the fabric is required to remove all the chemicals used before moving on to the next step. Once the process is complete, the water used is usually returned to the ecosystem without further treatment. This wastewater contains all of the process chemicals used during production. The type and quantity of these chemical

pollutants depends on the type of manufacturing facility, as well as the processes, fibers, technologies, and chemicals used in production.

Beyond manufacturing, the textile industry also uses an enormous amount of "virtual water." In 1993, Professor John Allan (2008 Stockholm Water Prize Laureate) introduced the "virtual water" concept, which measures the amount of water embedded in the production and trade of food and consumer products. For instance, the "virtual water" involved in textile manufacturing is the water that cannot be used for anything else because it is used up, evaporates, or becomes contaminated.

WASTEWATER

Textile wastewater (TWW) discharged by dye manufacturing and textile finishing industries is one of the most hazardous wastewaters for ecosystems when it is discharged directly into water streams without proper treatment.[62] As much as 65% of the chemicals used in the textile finishing process for cotton and 55% of the chemicals used for synthetics end up in wastewater.[63]

Dyeing and finishing are mainly responsible for the large amount of wastewater. Many dyes, including natural dyes, do not "adhere" to the fabric well enough to prevent a large amount of polluted water from being washed off the fabric after it is dyed. For instance, a fabric retains only about 80% of its directly applied dyes, while the rest is flushed out from the garment.[64] Although wastewater can be treated to remove dyes and toxic chemicals such as heavy metals, this treatment process is expensive and does not always occur.

Indonesia is a major contributor to the global textile and clothing industry. It is also home to the most polluted river in the world, the Citarum River. The river is named after a plant called tarum, which is extracted from the leaves or bark of native trees and used as a form of dye for the rare botanical blue dye, indigo. Traditionally, Indonesian batik makers used tarum in their batik textile processes, a method that entails using a wax resist to dye and produce colored designs on fabric.

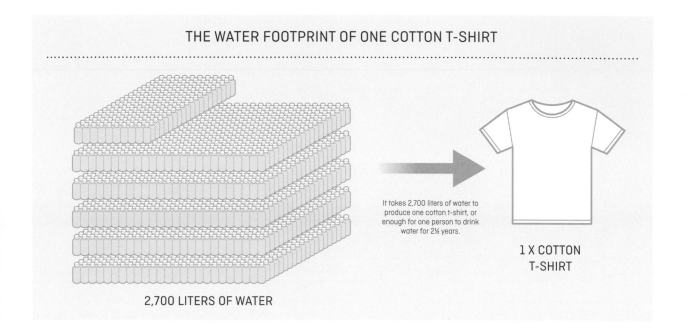

THE WATER FOOTPRINT OF ONE COTTON T-SHIRT

It takes 2,700 liters of water to produce one cotton t-shirt, or enough for one person to drink water for 2½ years.

1 X COTTON T-SHIRT

2,700 LITERS OF WATER

Today, the river is no longer home for the tarum plant that once flourished in the area, nor for the community that relied on its production. Rapid industrialization in the 1980s, a lack of waste management, and the rise of synthetic fibers have coincided with the river's hazardous pollution. As of 2019, there are over 2,000 industries near the river, most of which dump toxic chemicals, such as arsenic and lead, into the water.[65]

RECYCLED WATER

Efforts are being made by some companies to reduce the amount of wastewater in textile production and manufacturing. In partnership with their Chinese factory, Levi's® engineered a system to pipe 100% recycled water into an industrial laundry machine used for finishing one of its jean lines. The company is the first in the industry to use a new water recycling standard that reduces the impact on freshwater resources. The initiative started in 2014 with 100,000 pairs of women's jeans made with 100% recycled water. The result was a saving of approximately 3.2 million gallons (12 million liters) of water, enough to fill almost five Olympic-size swimming pools.[66]

LAND USE

The global textile and apparel industry requires a massive amount of land for raw material production and fabric manufacturing. Such land use has significant implications for biodiversity—the diversity of the earth's species that provide critical services such as pollination, water purification, and climate regulation.

ORGANIC LAND USE

The development of sustainable agricultural practices, such as growing organic cotton, will dramatically decrease the negative environmental impacts associated with conventional growing methods. Organic agriculture can also improve the health of both the land and the communities that rely on it by reducing their exposure to toxic pesticides which can end up in the soil, air, water, and food supply.

REGENERATIVE LAND USE

Regenerative agriculture involves a wide range of techniques that aim to replenish soil, restoring its biodiversity. Improving the health of the soil in this way helps remove CO_2 from the atmosphere. Luxury French fashion group Kering and holistic land manager the Savory Institute collaborated in the goal of expanding regenerative agriculture measures within the fashion industry and its supply chain. The Land to Market program advocates identifying and developing an improved network of farms that demonstrate positive ecological outcomes. Kering brands will be able to access these farms in their supply chains. The program aims to improve the industry's impact on the global environment by utilizing the Ecological Outcome Verification (EOV) certification. EOV measures positive or negative trends in the overall health of a landscape.

The expansion of the regenerative agriculture framework is a means to reverse environmental degradation through restoring healthy soil to the earth.

GREENHOUSE GASES

In December 2015, at the Conference of the Parties (COP 21) in Paris, France, specific countries reached a landmark agreement to combat climate change and to accelerate and intensify the actions and investments needed for a sustainable low-carbon future. The Paris Agreement's central aim is to strengthen the global response to the threat of climate change by keeping a global temperature rise this century well below 3.6° Fahrenheit (2° Celsius) above pre-industrial levels and to pursue efforts to limit the temperature increase even further to 2.7° Fahrenheit (1.5° Celsius). If the world heats up by the former, we could see mass displacement due to rising seas, a drop in per capita income, regional shortages of food and fresh water, and the loss of animal and plant species at an accelerated speed.

Research suggests that the world is not, however, on track to achieve the targets of the Paris Agreement. As of 2019, the total greenhouse gas emissions from textile production amounted to 1.2 billion tons annually. To keep the temperature increase below 2.7° Fahrenheit (1.5° Celsius) greenhouse gas emissions need to be cut by 45% by 2030 and a net zero-emission economy built by 2050.[67]

Wastewater management at the textile factory PT Kahatex, Indonesia.

The Fashion Industry Charter for Climate Action, launched in 2018, sets a target of 30% greenhouse gas emission reduction by 2030 and a commitment to analyze and set a de-carbonization pathway for the fashion industry drawing on methodologies from the Science-Based Targets Initiative. The Science-Based Targets Initiative is a partnership between CDP, a charity which helps organizations and cities measure their environmental impact, UN Global Compact, World Resource Institute (WRI) and the World Wildlife Fund (WWF) which helps companies set emission reduction targets aligned with what the latest climate science says is necessary to meet the goals of the Paris Agreement.

ASSESSMENT TOOLS

A good first step toward more circular processing is to use assessment tools to measure negative impacts and understand areas where improvements may be made along supply chains. By identifying and tracking chemical consumption, energy use, and water use in textile processing, a baseline can be created to improve human and environmental impacts or ensure that resources can be circulated.

IDENTIFYING TOXIC CHEMICALS

Transparency in supply chains is key to obtaining accurate information about chemicals used in products. Data will enable long-term scalable growth in the use of safer chemistry and circular product design. The ZDHC Roadmap to Zero Programme is a coalition of apparel and footwear brands and retailers working together to advance the industry toward zero discharge of hazardous chemicals. The ZDHC Manufacturing Restricted Substances List (ZDHC MRSL) records chemical substances that are banned from intentional use in facilities that process textile materials, leather, and trim parts used in fabrics, apparel, and footwear.

Detox to Zero is a reporting system based on the Greenpeace campaign Detox My Fashion, which asks fashion companies to stop polluting waterways with hazardous chemicals from clothing production. Detox to Zero/OEKO-TEX enables textile producers to assess the status of their chemical management systems with a practical and usable analysis and assessment tool that creates transparency and control in the use of hazardous substances.

ChemFORWARD is a nonprofit collaboration between fashion brands, retailers, and NGOs to advance better chemistry in design and manufacturing. MaterialWise, a project of ChemFORWARD, consolidates global regulatory lists to help producers quickly identify and eliminate known chemicals of high concern from the beginning of the design process. As a free screening tool, it also enables users to reference restricted substance lists to check for compliance with certifications and preferred purchasing programs.

Greenpeace's "Detox Catwalk," held in a polluted paddy field in Indonesia, in 2015, to highlight the toxic effects of the fashion industry.

Left: The ZDHC Roadmap to Zero logo.   **Right:** The Higg Index logo.

CONDUCT, VERIFY, AND SHARE ASSESSMENTS

The Higg Index is a series of sustainability assessment tools developed by the Sustainable Apparel Coalition (SAC), an industry-wide group working to reduce the environmental and social impacts of products around the world. The Higg Index enables suppliers, manufacturers, brands, and retailers to evaluate materials, products, facilities, and processes based on environmental performance, social labor practices, and product design choices. More than 8,000 brands, retailers, and manufacturers use the Higg Index tools, in a collective effort to improve supply chain sustainability across the global apparel, footwear, and textile value chains.

The Higg Materials Sustainability Index (MSI) assigns a score to materials based on their environmental impact from extraction or production of raw materials, through manufacture and finishing, to the final fabric ready to be turned into product. The processing score is based on the scores for the following impacts: global warming, water pollution, water scarcity, resource depletion, and chemicals. The MSI then adds a score for chemistry (which varies depending on the type of certification) and then yields an MSI score for the material.

CERTIFICATION

For a positive impact on human health and the environment, third party certification for materials being used in any fashion product is highly beneficial. Certification ensures credibility; rigorous, science-based assessment; alignment with global best practices and standards; and provides assurance for customers and external stakeholders. Bringing safe materials and processes into circular design work provides a great opportunity to collaborate, envision new partnerships, and invent better solutions.

THINK PIECE:
Consider an item of clothing you are wearing. Trace its origin. Was the fiber the material is made from once growing in a field, on an animal's back, or splashing around at the bottom of an oil well? Determine how many processes it took so you could wear this single item of clothing.

5: PEOPLE AND PRODUCTION

The primary factor used to distinguish developed countries from developing countries is a country's Gross Domestic Product (GDP), the total US dollar amount of all goods and services produced in a country in one year. Developed countries like the United States, Canada, Australia, the United Kingdom, and Germany, for instance, have significantly higher GDP and Human Development Index figures (HDI is a statistic used to measure life expectancy, education, and per capita income), technologically advanced infrastructure, and a more advanced economy compared to other less developed countries.

The human element in the fashion and apparel industries is difficult to ignore, with millions of people around the world employed along its value chain. Circular systems will have a significant impact on both the large fashion brands who control production and the low-income workers who produce their clothing. But it is not possible to achieve true circularity without building a strong social foundation. This starts with ensuring respect and dignity for all workers employed throughout the entire fashion industry.

THE GLOBAL ASSEMBLY LINE

Modern apparel manufacturing methods have become a global assembly line where production is easily dispersed. Companies in developed countries outsource to developing countries, while those in developing countries move production within and between countries to find the cheapest labor. Outsourcing is usually operated with the aim of saving development, production, and fixed costs.

Outsource: *to procure (something, such as some goods or services needed by a business or organization) from outside sources and especially from foreign or nonunion suppliers: to contract for work, jobs, etc. to be done by outside or foreign workers.*

Merriam-Webster Dictionary

Most of the world's garment production takes place in developing countries such as China, Bangladesh, India, Pakistan, Vietnam, Indonesia, Ethiopia, Sri Lanka, and the Philippines. While garment production offers much-needed investment and employment in less developed countries, competition among those countries ensues to offer the cheapest labor force with the most flexible and often unregulated working conditions. Negative outcomes from the current system comprise reinforcing low wages, insecure employment, long working hours, lack of worker empowerment, gender discrimination, and dangerous working conditions.

Transitioning from a linear to a circular economy in fashion has the potential to improve the environment and peoples' lives. The International Resource Panel, part of the United Nation's Environment Programme, has stated that using resources more effectively (as in the circular fashion model) could increase the size of the global economy by $2 trillion (£1.5 trillion) by 2050.[68] For instance, businesses that turn recycled materials into higher-value products are projected to offer a new wave of manufacturing processes and job opportunities.

PEOPLE

As the fashion industry strives to identify a myriad ways to "design out" waste, it also needs to "design out" the social injustice of the current system. While there has often been a focus on the potential environmental benefits of circularity, less attention has been paid to the creation of better lives for the workforce. A human-centric opportunity presents itself if people are put at the core of the circular fashion system.

Left: Relatives of Bangladeshi workers who lost their lives in the Dhaka garment factory disaster, in which 1,134 people died, protest in June, 2013.

Right: Embroidered activism from Bryony Porter @Tickover. A percentage of profits is donated to organizations like Labour Behind the Label and Extinction Rebellion.

Corporate social responsibility is not new, but as a new generation of consumers becomes aware of the industry's environmental, political, and social issues, brands are increasingly held accountable for what they are doing (or not doing) in the communities in which they operate. As Li Edelkoort, the celebrated trend forecaster, put it: "How can a product that needs to be sown, grown, harvested, combed, spun, knitted, cut and stitched, finished, printed, labeled, packaged and transported cost a couple of euros?"[69]

GARMENT WORKERS

A garment worker is simply a person who makes garments. Unlike a fashion designer, dressmaker, or tailor, who are celebrated and rewarded for their skills, garment workers are at the bottom of the manufacturing process. Garment workers may work in large factories as core workers or as contract workers for smaller companies. They may also work from home as subcontractors (authorized or unauthorized), shifting the burden of production costs from the manufacturer to the worker. Unauthorized subcontracting is a frequent problem in the current system. Some of the worst labor abuses occur in unauthorized subcontracted facilities without any kind of scrutiny or accountability.

Many garment workers are still exposed to hazards such as factory fires and the use of dangerous chemicals. Estimates suggest that around 27 million workers in fashion supply chains worldwide are suffering from work-related illnesses and diseases. There are approximately 1.4 million injuries in fashion industry workplaces each year—equivalent to an injury rate of 5.6 per 100 workers.[70] These workers—mostly women—have little or no power or job security, and often suffer discrimination.

A labor or trade union is a group of workers who have come together to make collective decisions about their working conditions and to protect their rights. Most garment workers do not belong to unions due to competitive pressures throughout the supply chain. In order to keep labor inexpensive, apparel manufacturers generally prefer their suppliers to be anti-union and typically do not allow for the unionization of their workers. To improve working conditions, therefore, workers must be empowered, allowed a voice, and have their most critical concerns addressed through fair and consistent processes. Worldwide, there are examples of how organizations, activism, and information awareness can collectively improve the lives of workers.

Fashion Revolution's "Who Made My Clothes" campaign aims to empower garment workers and challenge consumer behavior.

Left: Labour Behind the Label advocates for workers' rights worldwide.

ORGANIZATIONS

While a culture of mistreatment of people has yet to be fully addressed, unions, labor activists, and most importantly, organizations train workers themselves to act.

The Clean Clothes Campaign is the garment industry's largest global alliance of labor unions and is dedicated to empowering workers and improving working conditions by raising awareness of human rights issues in the global garment and sportswear industries.

The International Labour Organization, founded in 1919, is a UN agency that brings together governments, employers, and workers to set labor standards, develop policies, and devise programs promoting decent work for all.

Labour Behind the Label is a UK-based non-profit group that focuses exclusively on supporting labor rights in the global garment industry by publishing reports and raising awareness through campaigns.

The Solidarity Center, a US-based international worker rights organization, has trained more than 6,000 union leaders and workers in fire safety, helping to empower factory-floor-level workers to monitor for hazardous working conditions.[71]

The Worker Rights Consortium conducts independent, in-depth investigations. It issues public reports on factories producing for major brands, and aids workers at these factories in their efforts to end labor abuses and defend their workplace rights.[72]

IndustriALL represents 50 million workers in 140 countries across many sectors, including textiles, garments, leather, and footwear. It fights for better working conditions and trade union rights around the world.[73]

Left and right: By exposing inconvenient truths, Fashion Revolution demands change for garment workers.

ACTIVISM

Activism involves the use of forceful campaigning to bring about social or political change. The Who Made My Clothes campaign from the non-profit Fashion Revolution movement was precipitated by the collapse of the Rana Plaza garment factory building in Bangladesh in 2013. The campaign's mission is to unite everyone in the fashion industry, from designers and makers, to distributors and wearers, to work together toward changing the way clothing is sourced, produced, and consumed. The movement has gathered such momentum that alternatively worded posters such as "I Made Your Clothes" are now being used by the garment workers themselves to draw attention to the need for greater supply chain transparency.

INFORMATION AWARENESS

Making consumers and governments aware of the lives and working conditions of garment workers is also a means of drawing attention to the problems. The Garment Worker Diaries (GWD) is a research project with credible data on the work hours, income, and expenses of workers in India, Cambodia, and Bangladesh. The objective of the project is

to use the data to improve the lives of garment workers through government policy decisions, collective bargaining, and factory and brand initiatives.

LIVING WAGE

According to the Universal Declaration of Human Rights, Article 23: "Everyone who works has the right to just and favorable remuneration ensuring for himself and his family an existence worthy of human dignity."[74]

Families and individuals working in low-paying jobs often make insufficient income to meet the standards of the cost of living. Most garment workers today receive wages well below the living wage (the minimum income required to afford basic needs such as food, water, healthcare, clothing, electricity, and education for oneself and one's dependents). The payment of a living wage could transform the lives of millions of people along the fashion industry supply chain by helping them to lift themselves out of poverty and drive economic growth within communities.

ELLA PADS

Launched in 2015, Ella Pads demonstrates a positive circular solution to tackle serious issues of environmental waste, while simultaneously addressing social barriers faced by female garment workers. Bangladeshi female garment workers miss an average of three to four days of work and wages every month because they lack access to sanitary products and many factories do not have sanitary facilities for women. Using garment waste scraps from the Zahara Fashion Ltd. factory in Dhaka, Bangladesh, the company produces low-cost sanitary napkins and underwear. The key feature of the products is that they are made, owned, and used by female workers.[76]

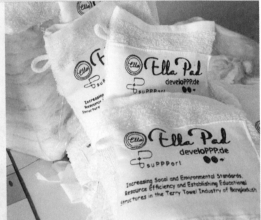

RESPECTFUL, SAFE, AND SECURE WORK ENVIRONMENTS
Many workers are not only exposed to safety hazards, but also subject to long hours and workplace discrimination. Two-thirds of the global garment workforce are female. Often, some of the higher-skilled tasks such as cutting are done by men, while women are tasked with basic work such as stitching. Where garments may require advanced technical skills to produce, women are replaced by men, who ultimately have more opportunity to learn new skills.[75]

PRODUCTION

Production is the process by which design concepts are made into a tangible and saleable product. In most cases, production begins with a small set of samples or prototypes and ends with commercial quantities of the item or style, often in multiple sizes, colors, prints, and patterns. The mass production of fast fashion has had a direct impact on the quality of every garment, from the textiles it is made of to the value of the finished product. While offering an immense selection for the consumer, the mass production of clothing has led to huge amounts of waste. Unused, unsold garments are not only polluting the environment, they represent huge financial losses for manufacturers, distributors, and retailers.

A growing number of small enterprises, as well as some of the world's largest fashion companies, such as Nike, Levi's®, and the luxury group Kering, have adopted circular economy commitments that have profound impacts on their suppliers and manufacturing processes. By replacing the rhetoric of broad corporate social responsibility (CSR) statements with transparency, and embracing the risks of innovative regenerative production methods, such as using recycled fibers to create new garments, they have become the frontrunners in the circular fashion story.

TRANSPARENCY

A fashion company's investment in the knowledge of suppliers along their supply chain remains a key pillar of a strong human and labor rights management system. To make certain that garment worker rights are being upheld, companies in developed countries need to know which factories in which developing countries are responsible for the production of their products. There is virtually no way of ensuring that the workers who make clothing aren't being exploited if the companies higher up the chain continue to remain ignorant of their suppliers.

An investment in transparency demonstrates a company's willingness to be accountable to consumers, civil society, and workers. It also makes it easier for these groups to collaborate to ensure that the rights of workers are upheld. A publication of a list of suppliers that includes supplier business names and addresses builds confidence among consumers who care about ethical and sustainable business practices. Supplier transparency gives workers hope that well-known companies will hear of their struggles and intervene to improve conditions. Regardless of the numerous benefits, supply chain transparency and traceability remains a voluntary measure in the current fashion supply chain.

For instance, Swedish direct-to-consumer menswear brand Asket developed a traceability score, grouping every garment into the four major categories of its creation: manufacturing, milling, raw materials, and trims. Each category is split into its individual sub-processes, up to six per category, which are traced and rated according to how much the company knows about the garment. The end result is a traceability score.

Traceability: *the ability to identify and trace the history, distribution, location, and application of products, parts, materials, and services.*
International Organization for Standards 9001:2015

SUPPLY CHAIN TRACEABILITY AND TRANSPARENCY INFORMATION TO BE SHARED WITH CONSUMERS:

Product information
composition, origin, manufacturer details

Social information
names and addresses of all suppliers, social certifications/inspections

Environmental information
carbon footprint, environmental certification, and recycling data

INFORMATION TO BE SHARED AMONG BUSINESSES IN THE SUPPLY CHAIN:

Product information
composition, origin, manufacturer details

Social information
names and addresses of all Tier 1, 2, 3 suppliers, social certifications/inspections

Environmental information
carbon footprint, environmental/social certification, and recycling data

Quality information
audit reports and test reports

Process information
related to process details, tracking, and specifications

Left: Supply chain traceability is provided on every garment from Swedish menswear brand, Asket.

Opposite: A tempting Gucci store display in Dubai. Palladium coating can be seen on the bag clasps.

ENVIRONMENTAL PROFIT AND LOSS

Some brands are beginning to assess their contribution to climate change, pollution, and water use, among other environmental issues, in financial terms. Current corporate accounting methods do not capture the impact and dependencies their company has on natural systems, so brands must find ways to quantify this information, taking in to account all their products. In 2011, Puma developed the first Environmental Profit & Loss (EP&L) statement, but it was the luxury group Kering that refined the methodology.

To facilitate the assessment of natural capital, Kering have created the EP&L accounting tool to measure, monetize, and manage environmental impacts across supply chains. Kering analyzed its environmental impact from raw materials to the delivery of products to its customers, including logistics and stores. Through its assessment,

a deeper understanding emerged of its activities, enabling better decision-making so as to reduce the group's detrimental impact. Kering published its EP&L methodology in order to provide an open-source tool to encourage other corporations to understand their entire impact on natural capital.

Gucci was the first brand in the luxury group to adopt the original digital EP&L and unveiled its own digital environmental profit and loss account on its own open-source platform. Gucci-Up is a circular-economy initiative focused on the upcycling of waste leather and textiles generated during the production process. Since 2018, the company has reused leather scraps—around 11 tons in the initiative's first year. In addition, 66% of palladium coating, a high-quality plating material used for Gucci's metal accessories, is now recycled and traceable.[77]

LOCAL PRODUCTION

Local production or near-shoring is when a company decides to transfer work to suppliers that are geographically closer—for example in neighboring countries. Geographical proximity may lower transportation costs and eliminate or reduce currency exchange rates, taxes, and tariffs. A shared culture can also ease communication, including a greater understanding of laws and legislation affecting business practices along the supply chain.

Shifting from the linear "take, make, waste" model of production to a circular economy would involve much more recycling, repair, reuse, and remanufacture of products. This in turn would increase the drive of private and public sector organizations to use locally sourced materials to take advantage of the opportunity for new revenue streams and more efficient supply chains. COVID-19 may accelerate this shift, as global supply chains become less feasible.

New near-shored industries can create new markets for circular products, with an emphasis on generating local material loops and shortening supply chains. Skilled jobs in local workshops and manufacturing plants can bring production closer to consumers. For this to increase, local governments and garment industries need to train the workforce in the skills and capabilities needed for advanced manufacturing.

Bringing production and consumption closer together has several key advantages besides shortening supply chains and creating local closed material loops—ease of communication and improved environmental and resource efficiency. Drawbacks, however, may be a competitive disadvantage to global production methods and higher labor costs.

INDUSTRY 4.0

In the eighteenth and nineteenth centuries, industry used water, steam, and electricity to facilitate mechanized production. In the mid-twentieth century, the third industrial revolution gave birth to electronic-driven information technology. The fourth industrial revolution, known as Industry 4.0, is driven by a convergence of technologies such as the internet of things, the Cloud, 3D (three-dimensional) printing, and automation, all of which have facilitated a whole new world of possibilities.

THE INTERNET OF THINGS

The internet of things: the networking capability that allows information to be sent to and received from objects and devices.
Merriam-Webster Dictionary

Smart devices offer an effective means of gathering, collating, and analyzing data that can directly enhance production processes and can be placed on the factory floor. For instance, by integrating digital automation into sewing machines, factory managers can streamline workflows, saving time and resources. If a sewing machine is suffering from a higher rate of needle breaks, engineers can rapidly diagnose the problem and discover the cause almost immediately.

THE CLOUD

Cloud Computing: the use of services such as computer programs that are on the internet rather than ones you purchase and put on your computer.
Cambridge Dictionary

Cloud-based technology can play an integral role in supply chain efficiency and can streamline processes by reducing excess inventory, markdowns (goods reduced in price), and landfill waste by making information readily available to share. Some technologies can deliver transparency from design to distribution, enabling apparel manufacturers to manage risk through data analytics and access real-time updates from their mobile phones. Google Cloud partnered with designer Stella McCartney to build a tool that uses data analytics to help brands estimate the environmental impact of production processes. Data comes from a number of sources to measure key points such as water run-off, soil quality, waste, and greenhouse gas emissions.

3D PRINTING

Since the beginning of the 2010s, 3D printing technology has brought a fresh wave of creative experimentation to runway shows and has great potential as a new mass-customization solution for consumers. The first 3D garments were presented in 2011 in a ready-to-wear show entitled "Crystallisation" by Dutch designer Iris van Herpen in collaboration with British architect Daniel Widrig.

3D printing: the manufacturing of solid objects by the deposition of layers of material (such as plastic) in accordance with specifications that are stored and displayed in electronic form as a digital model.
Merriam-Webster Dictionary

3D printing technology is now advanced enough to be widely used by sneaker brands such as Nike, Adidas, and New

Balance. For instance, 3D printing is employed to configure the structure of a shoe to maximize performance or print each sole according to the foot of its customers. The technology is also used for prototyping, to produce molds for complex or technical parts. Luxury jewelry houses like Cartier also use 3D printing to save time and reduce costs.

For the most part, 3D printing is used for producing rigid designs and geometric shapes. Creating garments using the technology presents one of the biggest challenges for designers to overcome, given that clothes need to be very flexible. To overcome rigidity, most 3D printed garments are built using mesh systems that are 3D printed individually and later assembled.

An environmental benefit of 3D printing is that it can take place anywhere, from a home to a retail store, thereby reducing emissions caused by transportation. 3D printing also only uses the material it needs layer by layer, so reduces waste. Traditional plastics are no longer the only material available; many biodegradable filaments are now made from recycled materials. Unfortunately, due to its slow production time and high energy demands, current 3D printing technology contributes negatively to greenhouse gas emissions.

AUTOMATION AND ROBOTICS

Many industry experts believe that automating (introducing automatic machines) and digitizing the production portion of the supply chain presents a major opportunity for manufacturers and suppliers. Some believe that factories of the future, known as smart factories, will be completely automated, self-servicing, and self-repairing systems requiring minimal human intervention. A reduction in waste, better energy use, and lack of labor-related issues are cited as benefits of automation. Automation may also enable manufacturers to deliver better productivity and efficiency.

While fast fashion clothing retailers famously reduced product life cycles and shortened lead times, in the future, robots may re-engineer the apparel industry by delivering faster, more personalized manufacturing driven by consumer demand, ensuring that there is less wastage from unwanted stock.

Lead time: *the time between the original design or idea for a particular product and its actual production.*
Collins Dictionary

Amazon is taking steps toward integrated systems designed to minimize manufacturing time by quickly producing apparel once a customer places an order. The company secured a patent which lays out an assembly line system of computer-controlled textile printers, textile cutters, and sewing stations. Another patent describes a system using fluorescent inks as a guide for cutting fabrics. The inks are invisible under normal lighting, but once the fabric is illuminated with ultraviolet light, image sensors generate instructions.

There are potential downsides, however. By embracing manufacturing systems that rely more on machines and less on humans, fashion companies can potentially speed up production, which may further shorten the fashion cycle, causing even greater negative environmental impacts. Automating a factory workforce can minimize concerns around labor conditions in their facilities, but at the risk of disrupting garment industries with job loss.

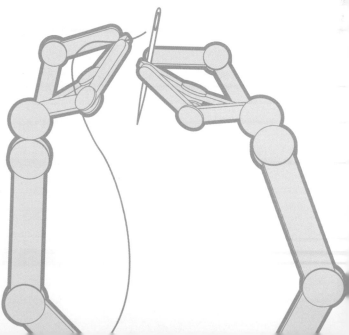

Above: A Sewbot® by SoftWear Automation at work.

Below: Nike's FlyKnit trainer, launched in 2012.

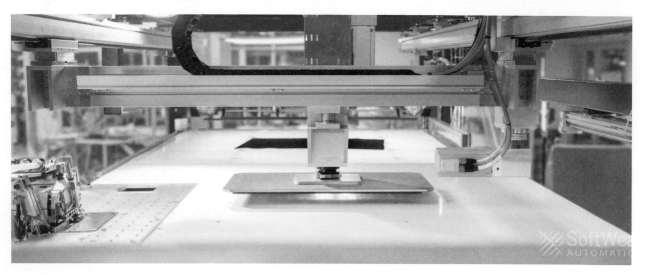

Technology obsolescence may occur as new technologies are designed to supersede older systems or when older machines cannot be repaired. Industrial machines require components that use rare earth elements, such as metals, flame retardants, and chemicals, which cause significant environmental impact from mining and disposal. If not properly recycled, they can leach into the earth, polluting soil and water sources. Human health may also be compromised because some of these elements are carcinogenic, causing diseases and damage to the nervous system.

SEWBOTS

Sewing, currently the most labor-intensive step in creating a garment, accounts for more than half the total labor time per item. The potential for labor reduction is highly dependent on product type and design: sewing a basic kimono top, for example, obviously takes less time and is easier to program than a tailored jacket with many seams. It is estimated, however, that as much as up to 90% of the sewing of simple garments can be automated.

The US-based robotic sewing company SoftWear Automation has developed fully automated Sewbot® robots. The innovation is in the cameras, which help the sewing robot track where the threads are at every moment and take corrective action if the fabric stretches or shifts. The company's digital T-shirt Sewbot® is fully autonomous and requires a single operator, producing one complete T-shirt every 22 seconds. The manual labor cost for a T-shirt is approximately 33 US cents (approximately 25 UK pence), while in the case of the robot that price falls to 5 US cents (approximately 4 UK pence).

However, sewbots may cause negative disruptions in the garment industry, particularly in countries like Bangladesh, Pakistan, and India. According to the Clean Clothes Campaign, up to 27 million jobs in these three countries could be at risk, specifically in Bangladesh where the garment industry currently employs 2.5% of the country's population.[78]

KNIT ON DEMAND

Advances in knitting technology, such as seamless, computerized, or 3D knitting, enable customization and

Future Finish in action as Levi's® uses a laser to finish a pair of jeans.

improvements in design and fit. These advances combined with open-source information on the internet have made customization of products more common in fashion design. It is possible to make garments "ready-made" directly in the knitting machine. A "knit on demand" business model, with production equipment in store, allows customers to be involved in the design process and finished garments to be customized to fulfil actual demand.

Nike's Flyknit product line employs a computerized knitting process using 100% recycled polyester, diverting more than four billion plastic bottles from landfills.[79]

FINISHING

While conventional printing techniques involve large quantities of water, chemicals, and dyes, automated finishing significantly reduces the use of these resources. Automated finishing techniques, such as digital printing and lasers, are resource-efficient, cost effective, and require little labor, which makes it easier to near-shore the finishing process. Levi's® uses lasers to create designs on its jeans digitally rather than with manual labor. The technique not only cuts out harmful chemicals, it reduces labor-intensive steps in producing jean finishes from 18–24 to just 3 steps.

REMANUFACTURING

The volume of production leftovers is systematically under-reported by companies and thus underestimated by the industry. Fabric production and pattern-cutting often generate huge quantities of waste. Pre-consumer waste refers to the scraps that are left over during industrial or manufacturing processes. Remanufacturing this textile waste has the potential to reduce factory spill (scraps left on the factory floor) and the total use of virgin fabrics from the production process. By remanufacturing products, materials, or parts a company contributes to the circular economy by extending the lifetime of these elements.

> **Remanufacture:** *to put (a manufactured material or product) through a process of manufacture again; to manufacture from recycled material or parts.*
> Oxford Dictionary

Reverse Resources is the first online marketplace to enable industrial upcycling for global fashion companies. It is a waste inventory service for large textile manufacturers and delivers information about their leftovers to brand designers, who can then trace pre-consumer waste through their supply chains. The platform recognizes three methods of reusing factory leftovers that can be applied in mass-production processes—invisible, visible, and design-led remanufacturing:

- **Invisible remanufacturing** uses leftover fabrics on the internal sections of a garment.
- **Visible remanufacturing** uses leftover fabrics on the external sections of a garment.
- **Design-led remanufacturing** is designing a garment with a specific waste stream in mind.

> **THINK PIECE:**
> Are robots the way forward? Discuss the advantages and disadvantages of robots replacing garment workers in the fashion industry.

REMANUFACTURING PROCESS

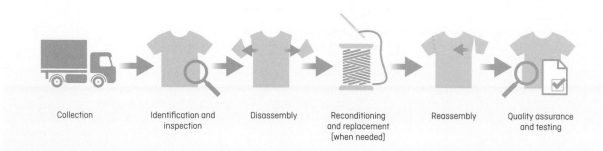

| Collection | Identification and inspection | Disassembly | Reconditioning and replacement (when needed) | Reassembly | Quality assurance and testing |

CIRCULAR LEADERS: CARRY SOMERS AND ORSOLA DE CASTRO

After the horror of the Rana Plaza factory collapse in Bangladesh, in 2013, Carry Somers and Orsola de Castro were determined to act. In response, they founded Fashion Revolution, a global activism movement (see page 83), with the aim of revolutionizing how clothes are sourced, produced, and consumed, helping the workers and the planet simultaneously.

The organization now comprises a team of volunteers who operate around the world, in every facet of the fashion industry. This enables them to have a wide reach and fight for change in some of the most deprived areas. A champion of the voiceless, Fashion Revolution has launched a series of successful campaigns, such as #whomademyclothes, which encourages brands to be more transparent about who makes their clothes and the conditions in which they work.

Prior to founding Fashion Revolution, both Somers and de Castro were advocates of a more ethical fashion industry. Somers' hat brand, Pachacuti, championed radical supply chain transparency, mapping the GPS coordinates of each stage of the production process, from the community plantations where the straw grows, through to each Panama hat weaver's house.

De Castro's career started as a designer for the upcycling label From Somewhere, which she launched in 1997 and ran until 2014. During this time, she collaborated with brands such as Speedo and Topshop, creating collections that used discarded textiles.

(fashionrevolution.org)

CASE STUDY #2: MAKE

MIRANDA BENNETT STUDIO: THE LOCAL PLANT DYE PRACTICE

Responsible fashion designer Miranda Bennett launched her first clothing line in New York in 2006, straight out of design school. She presented a sold-out trunk show of versatile clothing in convertible shapes, which led to multiple wholesale orders and a loyal following among independent boutiques. After a 12-year stint in New York, Bennett relocated her business to her hometown of Austin, Texas, in search of a more meaningful way to work within the fashion industry. The result is Miranda Bennett Studio (MBS), a clothing line that marries high-quality design aesthetics with circular production practices and environmental stewardship. Eschewing the built-in obsolescence model favored by many in the industry, MBS encourages a more conscious consumption by offering a core collection of styles that are available season after season.

The use of natural dyes is an important element of the brand's ethos. In Autumn 2018, for instance, Bennett brought her entire team to a commercial farm—Three Creeks Farm. Many years previously, Bennett had formed a farm-to-maker partnership with New Leaf, a non-profit social enterprise of the Multicultural Refugee Coalition, and they had worked together to train refugee families in organic, sustainable agriculture using community garden plots. It was now time to harvest the first crop of organically cultivated Mexican Mint Marigold (*Tagetes lucida*) from this agricultural partnership.

Working side by side with the refugee farm apprentices, the MBS team harvested the seasonal dye crop, gathering the plants with their tiny yellow flowers. These were then brought back to the studio, where the natural dyestuffs were prepared and soaked to extract the color. This soaking water became the dye bath, offering exclusive shades of citrus for apparel, accessories, and even nail color.

Although plant dyeing involves time and patience—some dyes require a lengthy steeping time, while others can just be crushed—for Bennett herself, it offers a way to "get [her] hands back into the process." Harnessing plant power successfully required a period of trial and error, but Bennett loved the "luminous and spontaneous" results she ultimately achieved. What's more, these plant colorways offered a unique opportunity to avoid the use of toxic chemicals and create garments with greater meaning for the wearer.

According to Bennett, the only disadvantage of this natural approach is "having to reawaken the lost knowledge of how to wear and care for naturally dyed apparel. The considerations for plant dyed items can be quite different than those of synthetic items: sensitivity to acidic substances or excessive sun, the evolution of a shade over time with oxidization, and so on. So much of our work as a brand is helping our customers to reframe their understanding of these characteristics, to know that they are not flaws, but rather an expression of the organic, alive quality of natural dyes."

Future initiatives include using zero-waste dyestuffs that are the by-products of other industries, such as sawdust, milled wood, avocado pits, and skins from local food suppliers.

DISCUSSION QUESTIONS

1. How does Miranda Bennett Studio contribute to the local community and the environment through local production?
2. What are the advantages and disadvantages of using natural plant dyes versus traditional synthetic dyes?

Above top: Connecting to nature by gathering marigold flowers that will form a natural dye.

Above: Natural dyes are formulated in small vat runs to produce sustainable colorways.

Right: The ethically made Cassatt Dress, designed for easy elegance and versatility.

Part 3
Market

CHAPTER 06: LOGISTICS AND TRANSPORT

Business Logistics: *the process of planning, implementing, and controlling the efficient, effective flow and storage of goods, services, and related information from the point of origin to the point of consumption for the purpose of conforming to customer requirements.*
The Law Dictionary

From farms to factories, great strides toward circularity are being made across different stages in the fashion supply chain. But a key part of the chain that often gets overlooked is how the products are actually getting from point A to point B.

LOGISTICS

"Logistics" is a word often seen on the side of a freight truck (haulage lorry) or cargo ship, but it can mean much more than just transportation. In the context of a fashion company, it describes the flow and storage of goods from the point of manufacture to the point of consumption. "Logistics" is used more broadly to refer to the process of coordinating and managing how resources are acquired, stored, and transported to their final destination.

THE FUNCTIONS OF BUSINESS LOGISTICS

Business logistics consists of various functions that have to be properly managed to ensure an effective and efficient supply chain. In the case of, for instance, an order for clothing garments, these functions can be categorized as follows:

1. **Order processing:** The order is accepted from the customer and is placed to the warehouse. If a retailer orders ten garments, the warehouse will automatically deduct ten garments from their inventory.
2. **Material handling:** Arranging the inventory of all the garments in an organized manner within the warehouse is important and allows for easy dispatch of the items.
3. **Warehousing:** Storing all the garments in a warehouse will allow them to be secured until they are sold or distributed at a later date.
4. **Inventory control** (also known as stock control):

BUSINESS LOGISTICS

1 Order Processing → 2 Materials Handling → 3 Warehousing → 4 Inventory Control → 5 Transportation → 6 Packaging

Continuously monitoring consumer demand of the garments ensures the garments are ready for sale.

5. **Transportation:** The physical delivery of the garments from the warehouse to the retailer or to the end customer may require a variety of transportation methods.

6. **Packaging:** Transport packaging is used to secure the garments and protect them against damage when transferring them from the warehouse to the retailer or end customer.

However much a company focuses on the design and production of their products to best meet their customer needs, the company will fail if those garments cannot reach their customers. Globalization, technology, and a speed-to-market model have led to the complexity of logistic processes across the fashion industry.

SPEED-TO-MARKET LOGISTICS

The current speed-to-market fashion industry has created time-sensitive fashion goods necessitating a fast-paced approach and product delivery model.

The seasonal fashion calendar requires a quick turnaround in order to create the extensive runway presentations in the traditional fashion capitals of New York, London, Milan, and Paris and increasingly in other geographic markets. Designs, materials, and samples have to be shipped to manufacturers and completed garments sent back to designers for approval and revisions in short time frames and under conditions of security.

When the styles of these new collections are ordered by fashion buyers, it becomes necessary to deliver the items in volume to retailers while the excitement generated by the media coverage of the fashion shows is still a relevant market influence. Additionally, there is competition from fast fashion retailers who are working simultaneously to produce the styles more cheaply.

Social media has also brought many changes in consumer behavior, and among these is the need for immediacy. A dress worn by an Instagram influencer or celebrity must be produced quickly and pushed onto store shelves instantly.

Fast fashion companies such as British online retailer ASOS, H&M, and Zara are built entirely on the speed-to-market idea.

While the fashion industry provides global consumers with new styles around the clock, the environmental impact of delivering goods as quickly as possible in "last mile" logistics cannot be ignored. ("Last mile" refers to the final step of the delivery process, from a facility to the end user.) The continuous flow of merchandise pushes consumerism to the brink and the constant use of international airfreight and road transportation modes generates high emissions of greenhouse gases.

Further complicating fashion logistics are fickle fashion consumers and relaxed return policies. Over the last two decades, online shopping has grown rapidly, making it possible to return unwanted merchandise without inconvenience or additional costs. Fashion Revolution's Highway Fitting video shows women trying on clothes on roadways to illustrate that while the act of trying on clothing at home is convenient and fun, the trucks which deliver fashion goods to consumers pollute the atmosphere while contributing to global warming.

PACKAGING

Packaging materials are a crucially important consideration when determining how to ship fashion products to consumers.[80] Plastic bags, paper envelopes, or cardboard boxes are generally the ubiquitous mailing options.

Paper envelopes or cardboard boxes may appear more environmentally friendly than plastic bags because they are made from a renewable resource, can biodegrade, and are recyclable. However, they require larger amounts of energy to produce than single-use plastic bags. On the other hand, plastic is a non-renewable resource and may take decades, even centuries, to degrade into the soil. Plastics also enter our waterways and pollute the oceans by breaking down into microplastics.

Surprisingly, many scientific studies show that plastic shopping bags have a much lower carbon footprint and global warming potential than paper and reusables, if the reusables are not reused multiple times. Many packaging and fulfillment houses offer recycled plastic mailing bags, yet these bags are still dependent on oil, a non-renewable resource.

PACKAGING RECONSIDERED

Thankfully, some companies are creating more sustainable packaging alternatives by rethinking these traditional methods. The Finnish company RePack, for instance, has created a way for e-commerce retailers to move away from single-use packaging materials. Inspired by the returnable bottle schemes of grocery stores, a company may post their goods using a RePack envelope made from recycled polypropylene, polyethylene, and cardboard. The envelope can then be easily returned by customers to RePack so it can be reused multiple times. As an incentive to return the envelope, customers receive a discount voucher to use at specific retailers who subscribe to the program. Once an envelope is no longer usable, RePack upcycles it into backpacks.

Duo UK is a plastic packaging manufacturer that produces recycled plastic bags and mailing bags using Green PE, a thermoplastic sustainable resin made from sugar cane.

PLASTIC HANGERS

Most hangers are made to keep clothes wrinkle-free as they make their way from factories to distribution centers, then on to stores and eventually consumers. "Garment-on-Hanger" (GOH) means factories and fulfillment houses ship clothing on hangers so retail store clerks (shop assistants) can hang up garments straight from the shipment, saving time. As a result, every article of clothing is already on a brand new hanger when it arrives. Therefore, when a piece of clothing sells, there is no reuse need for the hanger.

Temporary hangers, made from lightweight plastics such as polystyrene, are so cheap to produce that it is often more cost-effective to make a new one than to set up a recycling system. Since many plastic hangers are made of different and mixed plastics, they are hard to recycle. Separating the different types of plastic is difficult, if not impossible, on a rapidly moving recycling line. Recycling machinery is rough on materials and most hangers break into pieces before they even make the plastic separating section. Identifying chards of plastic is not possible.

It has been estimated that from eight to ten billion plastic and wire hangers are produced and sold every year. Of that number only 15% are ever recycled. Where do the rest go? Plastic hangers typically end up in landfills, where they discharge toxic chemicals such as benzene and Bisphenol A (BPA) into the environment. Wire hangers typically cannot be recycled by machinery.

French designer Roland Mouret collaborated with Amsterdam-based start-up Arch & Hook to debut Blue, a hanger composed of 80% plastic waste harvested from rivers with metal hooks. The hanger has a circular lifespan, meaning it can be continually recycled after use and the slate grey color means that it has not been tampered with by chemicals during the production process.

ROBOTS

As the speed-to-market fashion model experiences more demand for rapid fulfillment and accuracy, robots are providing safety, efficiency, and accuracy in logistics, mostly involving work in the distribution center. Robots can sort through incoming and outgoing packages faster, organize them on the appropriate shelves or shipping containers, and ensure the packages do not have any defects.

Collaborative robots (cobots) can be trained to do tasks by letting a human guide their arms once to learn the motion and to shutdown when they bump into something. Robotic software and 3D laser vision can view different products in a container and determine the optimal loading or unloading sequence with a high level of accuracy.

Japanese fast fashion retailer Uniqlo operates a warehouse in Tokyo which is almost entirely powered by robot technology. Large robotic arms can move sets of crates onto conveyor belts, or sort packages prior to shipping. The

Factory worker prepares cloth for a speed-stitching embroidery machine, South Africa.

robotic system is so effective that following the warehouse's technology makeover in 2018, robots replaced 90% of the human staff that worked there. The warehouse also has the potential to operate non-stop around the clock, except for occasional maintenance work.

As the fashion industry embraces automation, however, the risk of widespread job loss, particularly among factory workers, is substantial. A 2016 report by the United Nations' International Labour Organization (ILO) revealed that more than half of workers in Cambodia, Indonesia, Thailand, Vietnam, and the Philippines—at least 137 million people—could lose their jobs to automation in the next two decades.[81]

THIRD PARTY LOGISTICS

Third party logistics (3PL) involves using external companies to execute logistics activities that have traditionally been performed within an organization itself. Given the complexity of the processes involved, brands hire specialized logistics focused firms to assist them in expediting the movement of data, goods, and resources along their supply chain. Often apparel companies choose to outsource the management of their logistics to specialists such as Hong Kong-based supply chain manager Li & Fung Limited. Li & Fung Limited specializes in the supply chain management and distribution of high-volume, time-sensitive goods for leading retailers and brands worldwide. They digitalize each step of the supply chain so data can flow seamlessly, providing end-to-end visibility for their customers.

CIRCULAR REVERSE LOGISTICS

Adopting circular fashion principles has to fully account for the cost and complexity of logistics, disassembly, repurposing, and remanufacturing for a company to transition from the linear model. Reclaiming products and materials for future use means adjusting and modifying supply chains for returns.

Reverse logistics involves the collecting and grouping of products, components, or materials at the end-of-life for reuse and recycling, and also returns. It encompasses the collection of goods, transportation, and distribution to a central location, and sorting according to the ultimate destination—for instance recycling, remanufacturing, or disposal. It plays an essential role in closing the loop of a garment's life cycle and ultimately transitioning a fashion company toward circularity.

Take-back programs, warranties, and product defect returns all require reverse logistics to get the product from the consumer back to the manufacturer. Historically, if products were sent back to their manufacturer they were viewed as "heading in the wrong direction." For instance, customer return policies and how returns are handled have always been key concerns for retailers. The cost of processing returns using staff or additional resources, and the risk that the garments returned may not be easily resold, all have an effect on profit margins.

There is also an environmental cost. Optoro, a company that specializes in supply chain logistics, estimates that in 2018 alone five billion pounds of waste was generated through returns in the United States, contributing 15 million metric tons of carbon dioxide (CO_2) into the atmosphere.[82]

SUSTAINABLE RETURNS

Forty percent of online purchasers buy new packaging, often cardboard boxes, to return unwanted purchases. Happy Returns, an e-commerce service company, has developed an alternative which allows customers to bring unwanted merchandise to return locations, called Happy Bars, in reusable totes made from recycled plastic. The company estimates that the totes can be reused between 40 and 100 times, unlike single use cardboard boxes. A 2018 environmental impact study concluded that providing box-free return options for consumers reduces greenhouse gas emissions by 0.12 pounds per item returned.[83]

Greenhouse gas: any of the gases that are thought to cause the greenhouse effect, the steady rise in temperature of the earth's atmosphere caused by an increase in gases, especially carbon dioxide (CO₂), in the air surrounding the earth, which trap the heat of the sun.
Oxford Learner's Dictionary

EPR POLICIES

Today, as return flows are becoming more commonplace and textile waste piles up, Extended Producer Responsibility (EPR) policies (see page 155), which make a producer responsible for the treatment or disposal of post-consumer products, have been adopted worldwide.

Extended Producer Responsibility is a policy approach under which producers are given a significant responsibility—financial and/or physical—for the treatment or disposal of post-consumer products.
Organization for Economic Co-operation and Development

In France, for instance, one out of every five tons of material flowing through the economy is waste. France has reviewed available policy options and concluded that placing the responsibility for the post-consumer phase of certain goods on producers should be an option toward the reduction of waste.

Before setting up reverse flows, fashion companies need to evaluate their existing supply chain. Some obstacles they may face include complying with policies regulating the transport of waste, a wide geographic dispersion of returns, and the varying levels of quality and quantity in return loads. Cost and labor challenges are due to lack of scale, and sorting is both labor intensive and requires additional warehouse space. Some companies may consolidate their returns by combining loads with those of others.

TRANSPORT

Transportation is a key driver of economic and social development, reducing poverty, boosting prosperity, and achieving sustainable development goals. Transport infrastructure enables the supply of goods and services around the world; it allows people to interact and generate the knowledge and solutions that foster long-term growth. However, transport is one of the highest consumers of fossil fuels (produced from oil, coal, or natural gas), and accounts for about 64% of global oil consumption, 27% of all energy use, and 23% of the world's energy-related CO_2 emissions.[84]

> **Carbon emissions: *carbon dioxide that planes, cars, factories, etc. produce, thought to be harmful to the environment.***
> Cambridge Dictionary

If increasing volumes of fashion goods continue to move through scattered supply chains across the globe, demand for freight transportation will triple within a matter of a few years. We must rethink how goods are shipped with some urgency, or freight emissions will surpass energy as the most carbon-intensive sector.[85]

When planning transportation methods, companies can choose from a variety of transport options: road, sea, rail, and air.

ROAD TRANSPORT

Road transport is the most common and affordable option for the transportation of textiles and other light industry goods, such as clothes. Trucks are largely independent of railroad station, air, and seaport timetables, allowing for flexibility in delivery routes. Truckload optimization or "Full Truck Loads" (FTL) can reduce transportation costs, the number of deliveries required, and the impact on the environment: fewer trucks means less CO_2 emissions.

Even with optimization, however, the number of vehicles on the road worldwide is projected to double in the space of 30 years and thus reach three billion by 2050.[86] Motorized road transport causes air pollution and has been associated with

REVERSE LOGISTICS

1	2	3	4	5	6	7
End Consumer	Garments Reclaimed	Collection Center	Distribution	Recycle	Remanufacture	Refurbish Resale

a wide range of health conditions, including cardiovascular and pulmonary diseases. Black Carbon (BC), the sooty black material emitted from gas (petrol) and diesel engines, has recently emerged as a major contributor to global climate change, possibly second only to CO_2 as the main driver of the change. Each year, almost 185,000 deaths can be directly attributed to pollution from motorized vehicles.[87]

SEA TRANSPORT

Ships transport over 90% of goods traded worldwide. Shipping by sea is a popular option within the fashion industry due to the multiple geographical suppliers and producers of fabrics, garments, and accessories—large factories are scattered around the globe. Intermodal containers can be loaded to capacity, with unloading or reloading generating optimization and efficiency as the containers travel by different modes of transport.

Ships, however, are incredibly polluting. They emit sulfur dioxide, a pollutant linked to respiratory illnesses, as well as carbon dioxide and methane. Today, sea transportation is responsible for three per cent of global greenhouse gas emissions and nine per cent of transport-related emissions. If no preventative action is taken, the International Maritime Organization (IMO) predicts that maritime emissions could increase by between 50% and 250% by 2050.[88]

However, some shipping companies are taking action to reduce the environmental impact of their trade. For instance Maersk, the world's largest container shipping company, has pledged to become fully carbon neutral by 2050. Cleaner fuels are also expected to become less expensive as adoption grows and technology improves, and battery-powered electric ships are a feasible option for shorter distances.

RAIL TRANSPORT

Transportation by railroad is appropriate in the case of long-distance deliveries within a country or adjoining countries. High speed trains, adaptable passenger to cargo train carriages, and rapid trans-shipment (the transfer from one train to another) are benefits of rail transport. Trains follow strict timetables, so carefully planned delivery terms need to be agreed.

Trans-shipment: *the transfer from one ship, train, truck, etc. to another for reshipment.*
Collins Dictionary

Compared to other modes of transportation, freight rail has a relatively small environmental impact, with better fuel efficiency over long distances. According to the US Environmental Protection Agency, freight railroads account for just 0.6% of total US greenhouse gas emissions.[89] Shifting freight from motorized road transport to rail, therefore, offers a significant opportunity to reduce transportation emissions. It is worth noting, however, that railroad construction and freight movements can disrupt the habitats of wildlife.

AIR TRANSPORT

Speed-to-market supply chains and luxury haute couture designers may rely on cargo planes as a most expeditious option, but generally this is a very expensive method of transport for international delivery. The onward delivery of flown products can be handled from any international airport, and some brands choose to have their goods delivered directly to their warehouse or end customers.

The impact of the air transport industry on the environment is significant, with CO_2 making up approximately 70% of a plane's exhaust fumes.[90] While the International Civil Aviation Organization's 2019 Environment Report expressed a desire to reduce the environmental impact of their sector, air cargo has few options for transitioning to cleaner fuels, as the use of more sustainable "electrofuels" is currently minimal and not expected to improve quickly. A 2019 European Aviation Report stated that by 2040 CO_2 emissions are predicted to increase by at least 21% across Europe, provided mitigating factors do not intervene.[91]

Green cities must design
alternative, sustainable
transport systems.

GREEN FREIGHT

The transport sector still has a good way to go toward sustainable development principles in a circular economy, but solutions are emerging. Companies striving for sustainability and circularity will select safer, cleaner, more efficient, and accessible transport systems that reduce congestion and pollution, lower transport energy consumption, and perhaps even provide local jobs, all the while working toward the UN 2030 Sustainable Development Goals.

"Green freight" refers to a collection of technologies and practices that improve the efficiency of the freight sector and provide a means to help cut costs, track carbon, and benefit the environment.

A green freight program combines carbon accounting and disclosure with action plans, collaboration, and label recognition for businesses' efforts. The Global Green Freight Action Plan, launched in 2015, aims to develop and align green freight programs for over 50 organizations and countries worldwide, providing a platform for global and

regional cooperation.[92] The three main objectives of the plan are to align and enhance existing green freight efforts, develop new international green freight programs, and incorporate black carbon reductions into existing programs.

Green Freight Europe is an industry-driven program designed to help companies improve the environmental performance of their freight transportation across Europe. They have established a platform for monitoring, reporting, and reducing carbon dioxide emissions, and have also established a certification system to reward shippers and carriers who participate fully in the program.[93]

Carbon accounting: *the process by which organizations quantify their Greenhouse Gas (GHG) emissions, so that they may understand their climate impact and set goals to limit their emissions.*
Supply Chain Solution Center, 2019

GREEN FREIGHT PRACTICES

The following are some of the practices that can be used by the freight industry to reduce the environmental impact of freight transportation.

Optimization and efficiency

Optimizing vehicle loading, avoiding empty return journeys, and reducing the weight and volume of packaging creates efficiencies that reduce energy use.

Nearshoring and onshoring

Nearshoring occurs when an organization decides to transfer work to companies that are still less expensive but are geographically closer, thereby reducing the distance their goods have to travel. A US-based apparel company might move production of their jeans from either Bangladesh or China to Mexico, for instance.

Onshoring transfers a business operation that was moved overseas back to the country from which it was originally relocated. Closing the loop with direct links between producer and consumer in this way shortens transport distances and reduces overhead costs. Choosing local resources, products, and partnerships significantly reduces the need for long-distance transport.

Carbon efficient and multimodal transport

Using sea rather than air transportation, or rail rather than truck transportation, is more carbon-efficient.

Recycling end-of-life means of transport

Disassembling end-of-life transport equipment, reusing spare parts, and recycling the materials used to make them are essential. The Michelin Group is working to optimize tire (tyre) recycling—17 million tons a year worldwide. Through its Tire Recycling or TREC project, the company has developed new methods, including regenerating rubber compound blends to manufacture new, more efficient tires.

GREENER TRANSPORTATION NETWORKS

Modern transportation is currently experiencing major changes thanks to transformative transportation technologies.

Hyperloops

A new mode of transportation, proposed by Elon Musk, founder of Tesla Motors and SpaceX, is currently being designed and developed as a sustainable alternative to air travel. Hyperloops are essentially transportation tubes that run pods of passengers or freight through a pressurized track at high speeds of up to 760 miles per hour (1,223 km/h).[94]

FREIGHT DEMAND GROWTH IS MANAGED	TRANSPORT MODES ARE SMARTLY USED AND COMBINED	FLEETS AND ASSETS ARE SHARED AND USED TO THE MAX	FLEETS AND ASSETS ARE ENERGY EFFICIENT	FLEETS AND ASSETS USE LOWEST EMISSIONS ENERGY SOURCE FEASIBLE
• Supply chain restructuring • Localization and nearshoring • Decentralization of production and stockholding • 3D printing • Dematerialization • Consumer behavior	• Increased use of rail • Increase use of short sea shipping and inland waterways • Modular road transport • Cargo bikes • Multi-modal optimization • Synchromodality	• Load optimization • Load consolidation and asset sharing • Reduce empty moves • Modular packaging and boxes • Open transport networks and warehouses • Increase storage density and energy efficiency	• Cleaner and efficient technologies • Efficient vehicles and vessels • High capacity vehicles / duo trailers • Driving behavior • Fleet operation • Fleet maintenance	• Electric / hybrids • Solar / Wind • Biofuels • Hydrogen • CNG/bio-LNG • Cleaner diesel • Fuel management

Transport and logistic strategies for building a carbon-free future by Smart Freight Centre and ETP-ALICE.

© Smart Freight Centre and ALICE-ETP based on A. McKinnon 'Decarbonizing Logistics' (2018)   Roadmap Towards Zero Emissions Logistics 2050. ALICE (2019) www.etp-alice.eu

Futuristic hyperloops aim to transport people and goods in energy efficient capsules at high speeds.

Above: Temperature-sensitive road symbols communicate warnings to drivers in Daan Roosegaarde's Smart Highway project.

Below: Zero-emission high speed Maglev train prototype, Shandong Province, China, 2019. Maglev trains are guided by computer algorithms.

Smart roads

Smart roads, essentially roads enhanced with smart technology, represent an opportunity for sustainable energy growth. For example, a smart road could store solar energy and transfer that energy into electricity for vehicles and the surrounding infrastructure. Typical features of a smart road include being more animated and the ability to communicate with vehicles and people using sensors and data capture. The roads can also be responsive to changes in the environment.

Maglev trains

High speed maglev (short for "magnetic levitation") trains hover about 4 inches (10 cm) above their tracks and are propelled by electrically charged magnets. Maglev trains have lower CO_2 emissions due to their low energy use, and they can also run along existing transportation corridors which minimizes land consumption.

The trains have been recorded traveling at a rate of 375 miles per hour (600 km/h). A planned 2027 maglev train will transport passengers over 200 miles (320 km) between Nagoya and Tokyo in just 40 minutes, helping to free congested roads, lower air pollution, and reduce accidents. Maglev trains are in operation in China and Germany and are expected to become a common mode of transportation throughout the world within just a few years.

THINK PIECE:
How can innovations and technologies in transportation benefit our future circular fashion economy?

CIRCULAR LEADER: DAAN ROOSEGAARDE

Dutch inventor and artist Daan Roosegaarde's Smart Highway project incorporates a number of different initiatives to transform roads, from photo-luminating paint to reflective buildings. The project merges art and design with sustainable technology to envisage smarter infrastructure for the future which uses cleaner energy and increases efficiency for road users.

Furthermore, Daan has teamed up with the BMW Design Studio to think about the future of mobility and is a member of the NASA innovation team. He is also collaborating with the European Space Agency on his Space Waste Project, which involves upcycling space waste.

Young Global Leader at the World Economic Forum and a frequent lecturer, Daan regularly shares his visionary ideas for a greener, more sustainable world.

(studioroosegaarde.net)

CHAPTER 07: RETAIL

Retail has a key role to play in the circular fashion economy as millions of consumers buy their products in stores and online every day, and are increasingly interested in the social and environmental impact of these products. For retailers, this brings an opportunity to rethink the products they offer customers, build new revenue streams, and embrace business models that are good for people, the planet, and profits.

RETAIL REALITY

Technology has permanently shifted the way consumers purchase clothing and retailers engage with customers. Prior to the internet, for instance, consumers would purchase clothes in-store or through mail-order catalogs. Now fashion consumers are increasingly purchasing clothing online. Fashion apparel and accessories is the largest category of global online shopping overall.[95]

The rise of e-commerce and consumer demand for convenience and immediacy means that it is increasingly difficult to excite and inspire audiences who are often overwhelmed and overstimulated. Many retailers are suffering from the fatigue of a twentieth-century retail model that cannot compete with an online shopping experience. The old bricks and mortar retail store is becoming obsolete as it fails to adapt to a newer reality of retail in which consumers demand a wider selection of choice and more frequent stock updates.

Some of today's fashion consumers are looking for personalized experiences, unique local goods, and the ability to reduce their own environmental footprint. Some are purchasing products from retailers who advocate social and environmental responsibility, and they may even boycott retailers who behave contrary to this. Retailers who adopt circular fashion principles, such as offering the repair and resale of their own goods, will reach new customers and improve engagement with existing ones.

Given that many consumers still like to touch, feel, and try on clothing, retailers also have an opportunity to redefine the bricks and mortar experience with locally produced goods or personalized "feel good" moments that show a customer how their purchase kept waste from landfills or offset its carbon footprint. If retailers have an ethical standpoint, they can really bring it to life by showcasing that narrative in a physical space. Stella McCartney's Old Bond Street store in London contains air purifiers created by Airlabs, a pioneer in clean air technologies to reduce the effects of in-store air pollution. The store design showcases handmade, organic, ethically sourced recycled materials, reflecting the brand's ethos of fashion, luxury, and sustainability.

Retail: *the sale of commodities or goods in small quantities to ultimate consumers.*
Merriam-Webster Dictionary

CIRCULAR RETAIL MODELS

Circular retail models provide a template for retailers to create value while fulfilling new consumer demands and fostering sustainable growth and innovation. Fashion products and services, including resale and rental, that approach zero impact from an environmental perspective keep products in the retail economy. Refill or "package-less" stores reduce or eliminate packaging, and recycling of garments and textiles into future products closes the loop.

Circular retail models include recommerce, rental, subscription-rental, circular by design, and zero waste:

RECOMMERCE MODEL

Recommerce (reverse commerce) is the resale of previously sold items. Increasing the average number of times clothing

SECONDHAND EVOLUTION

1760–1840   Industrial Revolution

CHARITY SHOPS

1865   The Salvation Army Charity Shop is
            founded in London

1902   Goodwill Industries is founded in Boston, USA

1919   The term "thrift shop" is coined

1929–39   The Great Depression USA—The Great
            Slump UK

1937   Thrift Shop for Everyone Edinburgh, Scotland

1939–45   Second World War

1941   Red Cross Thrift Shop

1948   Oxfam Charity Shop

FLEA MARKETS, THRIFT AND
CONSIGNMENT SHOPS

1974   Buffalo Exchange opens in Tucson,
            Arizona USA

1989   World Wide Web is invented

1991   Thrift grunge looks of Nirvana

1991   ReStore Habitat for Humanity

1995   eBay and Craigslist are founded

2007–09   The Great Recession

2008   Actress Angelina Jolie wears a $26 thrifted
            dress on red carpet

ONLINE RESALE SITES

2009   thredUp, Vestiaire Collective are founded

2011   The RealReal and Poshmark are founded

2012   Hewi London is founded

2013   Designer Exchange and Grailed are founded

2014   LePrix is founded

is worn, recommerce is a well-established business model and the most direct way to design out waste and pollution while capturing the full value of clothing.

Recommerce models take time to get started because of the need to obtain used inventory and engage customers. Two ways in which pre-owned clothing is sold are through secondhand clothing platforms and take-back garment collection programs.

SECONDHAND CLOTHING

Clothes that were previously owned by another person are known as secondhand clothes. The perception of these garments has changed; used clothes are no longer seen as outdated, but instead customers place value on vintage products. A growing number of consumers are now willing to buy secondhand. Millennials (24–39-year-olds) and baby boomers (56–74-year-olds) do the most secondhand shopping, with Generation Z (18–24-year-olds) named the fastest-adopting group.

In the last three years of the 2010s, resale of secondhand clothes grew 21 times faster than traditional apparel retail, and the secondhand market is expected to reach $51 billion (£39 billion) by 2024 according to a fashion resale report from thredUP (a secondhand clothing retailer).[96] The unprecedented rise in secondhand clothes correlates with a rise in the consumption and poor quality of fast fashion which often moves from a closet to a donation bin frequently and in a relatively short time.

Secondhand clothing is sold in various ways:

- Pioneers in the secondhand market are traditional charity or thrift shops such as Goodwill, Salvation Army, and Oxfam, as well as flea markets and yard or car-boot sales.
- Resale platforms, online or as a mobile app—such as the men's designer and streetwear community marketplace Grailed in the US—offer consumers a global marketplace to like, buy, sell, or trade apparel alongside creative communities and curated social content.

   UPcycle, by secondhand clothing retailer thredUP, is an online platform that makes it easy for any brand to launch and scale a clothing recycling program. When customers send their used clothes to thredUP for resale, they have the option to get paid with a gift card to a partnered brand.

- Consignment shops, such as the online company eBay, provide an arrangement in which goods are left in the possession of an authorized third party to sell for a percentage of the sale. Such shops offer people a marketplace to present and sell their wares.

TAKE-BACK PROGRAMS

Take-back programs offer a satisfying retail experience by engaging customers in a cause and by bringing real meaning into a store trip. Pre-owned clothing is collected, sorted, recycled, or resold. Customers may receive a reward card for each recycled item or items, which may be redeemed against a purchase at the retailer's store or online. In some cases, if a customer does not live close to a store, they can send their garments directly to one of the retailer's recycling centers. Such programs can increase brand loyalty, entice new customers, and drive repeat purchases because consumers who bring in an old item to recycle often stay to shop for other products.

Take-back programs: initiatives organized by a manufacturer or a retailer to collect products or materials from consumers and reintroduce them to the original processing and manufacturing cycle.
World Business for Sustainable Development, 2019

There are two types of take-back programs: a non-specific take-back program, which collects all textile-based products from all brands; and a brand-specific take-back program, which collects garments purchased from a particular brand or retailer.

H&M Group has the most established and widespread non-specific take-back in-store recycling program. The Garment Collecting initiative was launched in 2013, with recycling bins in many of its more than 4,200 stores

COS's Restore collection gives life to damaged or unsellable garments.

worldwide. Customers can drop off a bag of clothing from any brand in any condition at their local store. Even odd socks, worn-out T-shirts, and old sheets are accepted. For every bag of textiles a customer drops off, they receive a discount card for 15% off their next in-store purchase. The collected garments and textiles are then sent to the nearest recycling plant. In 2018 alone, H&M Group, a Swedish company that consists of such brands as Weekday, H&M, COS, Arket, and & Other Stories reported that they collected over 20,649 tons of customers' unwanted old clothes and textiles.[97]

On the other hand, when brands implement their own brand-specific take-back program, they capture the total value of their own clothing, provide additional revenue streams, encourage deeper customer relationships, and create new sites for customer interaction, known as touchpoints. Products of high quality and durability are best suited for this program.

Left: H&M's in-store garment recycling bins encourage shoppers to donate unwanted items.

Center: Bags full of clothes ready to be sorted and washed, before being reused, at the Eileen Fisher warehouse in Irvington, NY.

Right: The ReMuji section of a Muji store in Bankok, Thailand, offers upcycled fashion made from recycled materials, scraps, and unwanted garments.

Renew is a take-back program from Eileen Fisher. Customers bring back pre-owned Eileen Fisher clothes in any condition and receive a $5 Renew rewards card for each item, redeemable online or at Eileen Fisher and Renew stores. In ten years, from 2009 to 2019, Eileen Fisher collected over 1.2 million pieces of the brand's clothing.[98] These items are then mended, cleaned, and resold on their Reworn site or upcycled into new designs under their Resewn Collection.

COS has initiated a similar project known as COS Restore, a collection consisting of unsellable or returned items that have been carefully mended and cleaned by Oregon-based The Renewal Workshop, making them fit to sell again. The Renewal Workshop operates a zero-waste circular system and works with fashion brands to recover the full value of apparel that they have already produced.

RENTAL COMMERCE MODEL

Imagine never actually buying your clothing outright, but only buying access to clothing. You would wear garments until you have grown tired of them and then exchange them for new ones. How would this influence the design of apparel or the logistics and tracking of fashion products?

In the context of fashion retail, "rental" means the one-off hire of a garment for a short period of time. Clothing rental has, however, quickly matured from this short-term, event-focused model to an everyday option for some consumers.

For companies with expertise in reverse logistics (see pages 102–03) and concerns about environmental impact, rental is fast becoming a modern way of accessing fashion. HURR Collective is a peer-to-peer rental platform in the UK that harnesses the same sharing feature that made Uber and Airbnb so successful. Built with an on-demand platform that uses real-time ID verification, geo-tagging, and fashion stylists powered by artificial intelligence, HURR Collective allows members to share their wardrobes. Members can rent in seven-day increments, for up to one month.

SUBSCRIPTION MODEL

Subscription models in fashion have grown exponentially in the last few years, driven predominantly by consumers who increasingly value convenience and access over ownership. Compared to traditional retail, subscription services enable consumers to try new items and to experiment in a flexible, low-risk way without leaving home. Three types of subscription models exist: subscription boxes, where clothes are purchased; subscription rental, where clothes are rented; and circular subscription, where clothes are either swapped and worn by others or recycled.

HURR Collective champions the rental model at their premises in Selfridges, London.

THANKS, IT'S RENTED

TRADITIONAL SUBSCRIPTION BOX	SUBSCRIPTION RENTAL	CIRCULAR SWAPS
Designed as a customer's personal stylist and to increase new and repeat clothing purchases.	Designed for personal wardrobe optimization with access to an online designer closet.	Designed for clothing returns and the re-use of materials.
Pros: Personalized shopping. **Cons:** New or repeat clothing purchases leading to more textile waste.	**Pros:** Renting clothing that is designed for longevity and durability prolongs the life cycle of a garment. **Cons:** Cleaning and shipping costs.	**Pros:** Circular or secondhand clothing including waste is looped back into the supply chain. **Cons:** Shipping and return costs.
Examples: Stitch Fix, Armoire, Lookiero	**Examples:** Rent the Runway, Girl Meets Dress	**Examples:** For Days and Circular Wear

For instance, the Danish clothing company Vigga identified a problem most new parents face: their child is less than four months old and has already outgrown two rounds of clothing sizes. The company offers a subscription service that allows parents to dress their children in high-quality, designer clothing made from sustainable materials that has been returned by other customers. Clothes can be exchanged when they are outgrown, avoiding unnecessary cost and waste, and ensuring a low environmental impact.

The environmental impact of subscription rental will, however, be especially important to watch as the model is scaled up. By offering convenience there is the potential risk that overall clothing consumption could increase. If these newer models are only supplementary to existing consumer purchasing in a linear model, this will increase production and waste.

In a subscription model, the customer churn rate (rate at which customers leave or join) is important. A high churn rate (customers leaving) could adversely affect profits and impede growth. Retailers can try and reduce churn through price point, convenience, number of garments, and additional incentives—for example, through exclusive offers.

Churn: a regular, quantifiable process or rate of change that occurs in a business over a period of time as existing customers are lost and new customers are added.
Merriam-Webster Dictionary

CIRCULAR BY DESIGN MODEL

As we have seen in Chapter 2 (see page 22), one of the primary reasons garments are not kept in circulation is that they weren't designed to be circular in the first place. As companies build systems to encourage more circular design, new technologies and circular business models will continue to transform the retail sector.

Identifying circular product characteristics (biodegradability, longevity, durability, etc.) can help retailers prioritize which products may be suitable to which model. Based in Los

THE SWAP MODEL: DESIGNED FOR CIRCULARITY

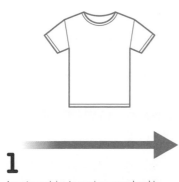

1
A customer joins to receive a membership. (Membership fees may be based on number of items the customer wishes to receive.)

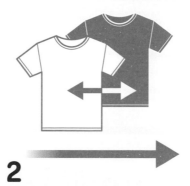

2
Whenever the customer is ready for something new, they can swap any item at any time for a small fee.

3
When the customer receives their new item(s), they send the older ones back to the retailer so they can be recycled into new items.

RENT THE RUNWAY

Rent the Runway, founded in 2009, is the most established subscription fashion service to rent out designer styles for everyday and occasion. Rent the Runway offers two membership plans: RTR Update is a once-a-month shipment of a minimum of four items chosen by the customer, and RTR Unlimited offers the same but with the opportunity to exchange these items for something new whenever the customer wants. The items are sent dry-cleaned and ready to wear in a reusable garment bag. When the customer is ready for something new, they can ship the items back in the garment bag they came in. RTR notifies the customer when they have received the return, allowing them to select something new for their next shipment.

Angeles, For Days creates circular garments with a closed-loop manufacturing and recycling process. The process is enabled by an organic T-shirt membership program that lets customers mail back worn T-shirts for recycling in exchange for new ones. The old biodegradable T-shirts are mechanically recycled and a new T-shirt is produced from the same materials, enabling customers to switch styles, colors, and sizes in a sustainable manner.

ZERO-WASTE RETAIL MODEL

Small retailers can take advantage of the more flexible nature of their business model by creating processes around waste reduction. Zero-waste processes recover the full value out of products that have already been created or encourage waste prevention, while offering consumers more incentive to shop local or close the loop.

Zero-waste stores also satisfy a growing desire to respond to consumers' awareness of the negative impact of textile and packaging waste. Some shops aim to end packaging waste by doing away with packaging altogether, while others may sell products made with eco-friendly materials.

The label for a cotton T-shirt by For Days, a brand that invites customers to swap and return zero-waste basics made from circular materials.

Helsinki-based brand Pure Waste produces garments from industrial waste.

Retailer Pure Waste is based in Helsinki, Finland, and was born from the zero-waste idea of making fabric from recycled materials. The company buys leftover scraps or waste cuttings from a textile factory in India, cuts it up mechanically, and mixes it with recycled polyester from plastic bottles to create a collection of mixed basic items. The clothing is manufactured at Pure Waste's own factory in India, where employees enjoy long-term work contracts and salaries that are double the region's average.

THINK PIECE:
As new circular fashion products enter the marketplace, what types are best suited for specific circular retail models?

KRISTY CAYLOR

Kristy Caylor is an entrepreneur, fashion visionary, and humanitarian. Prior to starting For Days, Caylor founded Maiyet, a pioneering luxury brand that integrated world-class design with a transformative social philosophy. Deeply committed to sustainability, Caylor was also an early innovator with Gap's Product (RED) and has served on the leadership committee for Cradle to Cradle's Fashion +. She was honored by the Voss Foundation as the 2014 Woman Helping Women Honoree and regularly participates with the UN Foundation. In 2016, Caylor was appointed to the World Economic Forum's Global Future Council on Consumerism. Since launching For Days in 2018, Caylor was appointed to the Glossy 50: Fashion Digital Front Runners, and For Days was named as one of Fast Company's World Changing Ideas.

(fordays.com)

CHAPTER 08: MARKETING

What are your views on sustainability? How should a clothing brand's marketing messages be communicated to encourage users like yourself to choose circular fashion products?

SUSTAINABILITY MARKETING

The three pillars of sustainability that comprise a sustainable development plan are social, environmental, and economic—often referred to as the triple bottom line (people, planet, profit). Some brands may focus solely on the environmental impact of their products and services, while others may emphasize social sustainability, such as creating a green space to promote the well-being of their workers.

Today, 75% of consumers around the world view sustainability in the fashion industry as either very important or extremely important, as reported in the 2019 Pulse of the Fashion Industry Report from the Global Fashion Agenda in Copenhagen, Denmark.[99] Marketing and communication play a vital role in educating consumers and convincing them of the importance of sustainable consumption and making circular fashion mainstream.

Marketing: *the business activity that involves finding out what customers want, using that information to design products and services, and selling them effectively.*
Cambridge Dictionary

Sustainability marketing is any marketing activity that uses the sustainable aspects of a brand's product or service to communicate or influence customers. It can be used as a tool to educate existing customers or convert new ones in measurable and meaningful ways. For instance, a brand may communicate to customers the type of materials or circular processes it uses or how it treats or pays its workers.

Marketing sustainability considers both the long-term strategic planning of a company and society's long-term interests. A brand with a commitment to environmental sustainability must first incorporate sustainable practices, such as transparent supply chains or responsible sourcing, in its business model before it can promote sustainability. A brand with a commitment to social responsibility must incorporate living wages and better working conditions.

As consumers begin to demand more visible and concrete information from brands about clothing, marketers must devise alternatives to planned obsolescence and communicate beyond the corporate social responsibility (CSR) strategies that most of them already have in place.

Corporate Social Responsibility: *a company's sense of responsibility towards the community and environment (both ecological and social) in which it operates. Companies express this citizenship (1) through their waste and pollution reduction processes, (2) by contributing educational and social programs, and (3) by earning adequate returns on the employed resources.*
Business Dictionary

Sustainability marketing begins with authenticity. For instance, as a new group of influencers, Generation Z (those born between 1995 and 2010) are the first consumer cohort to be brought up with technology and vast amounts of information at their disposal. In general, they are more practical and analytical about their decisions than previous generations and use their purchasing power to support causes they believe in, such as sustainability, ethical consumption, and climate change. This generation is also savvy enough to recognize the difference between a flashy advertising campaign and a genuine, long-term commitment to sustainability from fashion brands.[100]

If a brand's sustainability message is, therefore, to be believed by consumers, sustainability should permeate every aspect of its activity, from the products it makes to the resources it uses. A sustainable brand should offer transparency by sharing specific information about these aspects, together with what it has already accomplished and when it hopes to reach any new goals.

GREENWASHING

Greenwashing: *expressions of environmentalist concerns especially as a cover for products, policies, or activities.*
Merriam-Webster Dictionary

Can you tell the difference between brands that market themselves as sustainable and ones that actually make sustainable products? A company that leads people to believe it is doing more to protect the environment than it really is may be "greenwashing." Practices include a brand spending more time, money, and effort on advertising and marketing its image, products, or employees as "green," rather than working toward minimizing any negative impact on the environment.

Greenwashing emerged in the 1980s, a period when most consumers received their news from television, radio, and print media. These limited information sources, coupled with unlimited corporate advertising, permitted companies to represent themselves as environmental stewards when in fact they were actually engaging in unsustainable practices. "Eco-friendly," "organic," "natural," "biodegradable," "compostable," and "green" are some examples of the widely used labels that can be confusing and misleading to consumers. The environmental group Greenpeace launched

the website Stop Greenwash in 2008 to confront the greenwashing campaigns of companies and hold corporations accountable for the impacts their business decisions have on the environment.

SUSTAINABILITY OR HYPE?

The challenge for consumers is to distinguish between brands that are making serious, company-wide commitments to sustainability, and those that are making more superficial tweaks. But how easy is it to spot which ones are just hype? For instance, a brand may launch a small capsule collection that is made from recycled polyester or organic cotton, and that initiative then gives the entire company a halo of sustainability, when, in fact, the capsule collection makes up only a fraction of the company's product lines. Sustainability should be the starting point for everything a sustainable brand does. A sustainable brand is one that has successfully integrated environmental, economic, and social issues into its entire business operation.

When consumers look for sustainable brands, they begin with a brand's website to learn more about its business practices and processes. Genuine sustainable marketing places value on long-term loyalty. For example, successful sustainable brand Patagonia, an American outdoor clothing company founded by Yvon Chouinard in 1973, uses its website and social media to continue building the brand's ethical and environmental message, developing a community for like-minded customers rather than just promoting its products for short-term gain.

A sustainability marketing plan entails the following:

1. Designing products with circularity as a starting point. Good design is effective and efficient in fulfilling its purpose. Fashion products designed with modernity and aesthetic values combined with circular approaches, such as longevity, durability, and biodegradability, lay the foundation for creating authentic marketing strategies for sustainability.
2. Connecting customers with sustainability credentials by

using industry tools such as labels, standards, and certifications.

3. Using simple and direct communication. Sustainability messaging can be educational, but too much information using vague terms, concepts, or sensational facts and headlines, can overwhelm customers.

4. Engaging customers by sharing stories so the narrative resonates and empowers them to purchase products and brands that support sustainability.

5. Keeping "bragging rights" to a minimum. Not every sustainable initiative a brand accomplishes needs to be announced. It is not enough to produce one sustainable fashion collection and then revert to old practices, nor is sustainability a rivalry between brands to gain a competitive advantage.

6. Using ethical messaging. This means a brand being honest and accurately informing customers about products and their impact on the environment or community.

7. Creating an authentic brand culture that values sustainability in every facet of the business. Customers may research a brand to see how it is contributing (or not contributing) to the environment or its employees and community.

Some questions to consider when researching a genuine sustainability marketing plan for any brand are:

- Does the brand use mostly organic, recycled, or biodegradable materials?

- Does the brand report on its own carbon footprint with solutions in place?

- Does the brand allow customers to repair its products and then eventually recycle the products through a take-back program (see page 112)?

MARKETING "CIRCULAR FASHION"

If a fashion brand is to flourish, consumers must like the image that the brand creates in their minds. For decades, fashion brands relied solely on marketing strategies based on consumers' emotional needs to look good and to belong. The brands set strict standards for stereotypical ideals of appearance and often sold an unattainable lifestyle.

Fashion advertising reflects societal trends and pop culture. Celebrities are often seen as the manifestation of success—rich, beautiful, and perfect. Celebrity endorsements strengthen brand recognition and make consumers eager to wear the clothing of their favorite actor or pop star. The message to the consumer is that if you wear this garment or buy this product, you too can be part of this lifestyle.

Above all, and beyond advertising strategies, it is the brand's responsibility to be credible in the eyes of the consumer. As a response to consumer demand for more environmental and ethical clothing, brands may scramble to use buzzwords like "sustainability," or look for an easy way to appear "green." Credibility is at the heart of circularity. As discussed in the following sections, there is a lot of opportunity for brands to develop compelling, cool, and circular narratives that are different from traditional fashion messages.

SAVE THE WORLD/DON'T SAVE THE WORLD

World-saving marketing messages that shame consumers or make them feel bad about buying non-ethical clothing can actually be counterproductive. Once fashion consumers learn that nothing changes quickly in the industry, they may feel disappointed that their sustainable purchases have failed to produce immediate results. When marketing sustainability, brands should not rely on shock tactics, but should deliver messages that show how fashion can be both exciting and responsible at the same time.

New fashion brands coming to the market with clothing alternatives produced under ethically acceptable conditions are aiming to gain interest with more novel approaches, such as dressing with purpose or in protest. Ethical fashion promotes serious issues: good working standards and

A blouse from Birdsong's SS20
collection. All Birdsong's clothing
is made-to-order by low income
migrant women who earn a London
living wage.

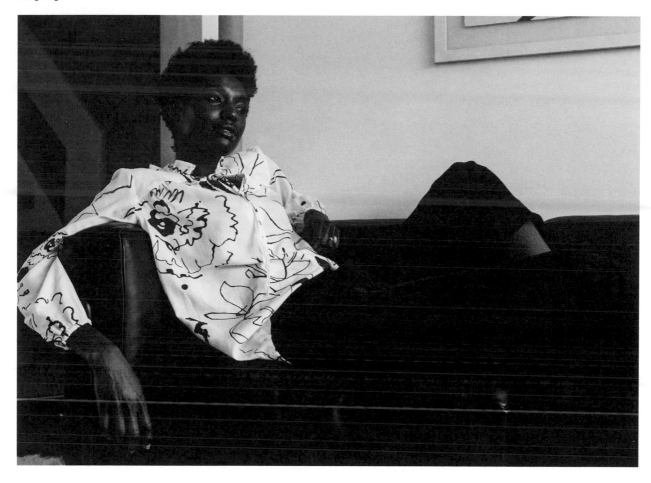

conditions for workers, and sustainable business models in the country of origin. Communicating social issues in clever but practical ways makes sustainability more relatable, less preachy, and accessible to the everyday fashion consumer.

Smaller start-ups can be the most daring with their sustainability communication. They do not have the task of transforming outdated business models or broken supply chains. Larger brands have to be more cautious in their messaging as they must answer to serious supply chain issues such as labor rights, low wages, dangerous working conditions, and pollution.

The London brand Birdsong states that "wearing our collection of original wardrobe staples is a protest in itself—against the fast nature of the fashion industry, against the obsessive pursuit of trends and against the systematic abuse of women in the production line."[101] Collina Strada, founded by designer Hillary Taymour in New York, is a collection of handmade modern and vintage styles which considers itself not just a fashion label, but a platform for social issues. It encourages customers to look inward by posing the question "What is your purpose?" These types of marketing messages capture interest in the brand and nudge consumers to act— to resist or to rethink their traditional buying habits.

New York-based clothes brand and social-change platform Collina Strada seeks to encourage self-reflection and self-expression.

GOOD HUMOR

If a brand can make people laugh and get them to genuinely enjoy themselves, social media sharing, word of mouth recommendations, and sales will naturally follow. Adopting a playful approach to marketing and communication without distracting from the seriousness of the message particularly appeals to technology driven consumers.

In 2009, Yael Aflalo launched her direct to consumer sustainable clothing brand Reformation with the tagline "Being naked is the #1 most sustainable option. We're #2." Described as "the ultimate cool girl brand,"[102] the Los Angeles-based brand reinvented the image of sustainable fashion by implementing a sense of humor—a unique selling point (USP) right alongside issues such as living wages, environmental impacts, and supply chain transparency.

Memes are videos or photographs embellished with text that poke fun at a cultural symbol or social issue and are transmitted rapidly by internet users. There is virtually no subject matter that cannot translate into relatable viral content. Instagram posts mocking unethical consumption habits and throwaway fashion can be an effective way to raise awareness of the brand itself and sustainable consumption.

Birdsong's memes use humor to promote their brand.

CIRCULAR NARRATIVES

One of the best ways to grow a sustainable brand is to create a personal and compelling narrative that showcases the brand's commitment and effort toward sustainability. Marketing narratives are used as tools to engage and interact with consumers.

A narrative is a story that must grab an audience's attention and introduce it to a series of related experiences, events, characters, or settings. In fashion, a circular narrative stays true to who the brand is, describes the brand's circular products, processes, or initiatives, and motivates consumers to deeper levels of action and citizenship, while perhaps sprinkling in surprise and delight.

Some fashion brands focus on storytelling to create a sense of overall authenticity. One of the most creative is Toqa, which produces sustainable fashion using all the fun, history, and folklore that make up island life in the tropics. Focusing on tongue-in-cheek humor, the branding reinterprets the stereotype of the aloha-shirt-wearing "Island girl." The collection is also closed loop—it uses rescued deadstock manipulated to reflect the brand's unique character.

Manila-based brand Toqa crafts
a witty narrative based on the
adventures of island life.

Deadstock: *a catchall for fabric and clothing that was never purchased by a consumer.*
Business of Fashion

Toqa's online experience encourages customers to take a "trip" to Manila featuring snippets of famous landmarks, including a souvenir shop comprised of the brand's best-selling items. By focusing on the brand's stories, it is able to bypass telling people how to behave, in turn creating an empowering, adventurous tone rather than a preachy one.

POSITIVE CONNECTIONS

If you want people to act, you need to appeal to their emotions. Feelings and emotions lie at the heart of the world's most loved brands. Positive intentions, attitudes, and behaviors within and outside the company give consumers the feeling that something is unique, positive, and memorable about the brand. Brands that have a reputation for doing good and being socially responsible in areas such as philanthropy, human rights, and environmental issues have the potential to help consumers make better and more conscious choices about the fashion products they buy.

CIRCULAR ECOSYSTEM

As a brand becomes circular, there is an opportunity to invite customers to join its community by offering teachable moments through lectures or workshops, transparency in its business practices, and relatable information about its "remade, reduced, and recycled" processes.

Entering a brand's circular ecosystem encourages a fashion consumer to learn about circular products and services, and to rethink their buying habits, perhaps allowing room for mended, renewed, or remade garments in their lifestyle. Trained and knowledgeable sales personnel are also a key component of community building, interfacing with customers through sales or public events, and giving extra credibility to the brand.

Story mfg.'s Grateful Long Sleeve
Tee in Mother Earth Bark Ripple.

STORY MFG.

Founded by a husband and
wife team in London in 2013,
Story mfg. (short for
manufacturing garments)
was born "out of a desire for a
more authentic, fulfilling and
kind approach to fashion—one
that doesn't involve a trade-off
between aesthetics and
consciousness."[103] The brand
combines new and traditional
slow fashion techniques

along with organic, natural fabrics to create cruelty-free,
vegan biodegradable clothing.

Story mfg. creates a meaningful connection between
customers and its brand by spreading the positive messages
with their "Slow Made" tagline and core values of honesty
and transparency in their unique, cleverly crafted Positive
Product Manifesto.

THE POSITIVE PRODUCT MANIFESTO (storymfg.com)[104]

Clothing is skincare
If the chemicals in clothing were packaged into a cream
you'd never let it anywhere near your skin.

Patron of the arts
We aim to... promote artistic practices and foster new
ones in places where people have been marginalized.

Waste is lazy
There is no "waste" in nature.

Animal kind
We never, ever, use animal products because we don't
feel there is anything sustainable or positive in raising
and slaughtering other creatures.

Regenerative agriculture
Our greater goal is to help reverse the damage done by
industry and enter into practices that leave the planet
better off after our work is done.

Family values
Our work is heavily craft-based... We are invested in
giving continuous, well-paid work and do not switch
for cheaper alternatives.

CIRCULAR LEADERS: SOPHIE SLATER, SARAH NEVILLE, AND SUSANNA WEN

Sophie Slater and Sarah Neville launched Birdsong,
a sustainable fashion label and social enterprise with
the ethos of "No Sweatshop, No Photoshop," in 2014.
Susanna Wen joined the team in 2017.

A commitment to collaborating with women makers
from local community groups who face barriers to
employment is central to the brand's identity. Their
expert team are paid the London Living Wage, and the
brand has raised more than £100,000 for women's
organizations across London since its inception.[105]

Birdsong's garments are made-to-order and crafted
with sustainable materials and reclaimed materials
from the UK-based textile recycling charity TRAID.
The company is also committed to using diverse
models, photographed by women or non-binary
photographers in order to eradicate the male gaze,
and a model's appearance is never digitally altered.
Birdsong sells on its own website in 28 countries.

(birdsong.london)

THINK PIECE:
After a proper analysis, determine if your
favorite clothing brand is truly a sustainable
brand or if it is just greenwashing. Are you
surprised by the results?

CASE STUDY #3: MARKET

VEJA: THE COOL SUSTAINABLE SNEAKER

Sneakers are the shoe choice of our time, the ultimate statement for workouts, workplaces, and modern lifestyles in general. But sneakers also carry a large environmental footprint due to their manufacturing complexities. They typically comprise synthetic materials, large amounts of non-biodegradable plastic components, and environmentally toxic glues, all of which make recycling impossible. Many conventional sneakers are also trend-driven, meaning they are often purchased and then discarded by consumers before completing their full life cycle.

Veja is a French brand that has carved out a unique niche and proved with its range of minimalist sneakers that combining style and sustainability can be chic. The brand was founded in France in 2005, three years after founders Sébastien Kopp and François-Ghislain Morillion established a non-profit organization that studied corporate social responsibility policies issued by companies around the world.

Working to reinvent the ubiquitous sneaker by using only ecological materials, the pair began working directly with small producers in Brazil. The rubber for their sneaker soles, for instance, is sourced from sustainable rubber tappers in the Amazon rainforest. Similarly, the brand's water-repellant V-12 Mesh model is made from recycled plastic bottles that are collected from the streets of Rio de Janeiro and São Paulo, where they are sent to a local factory to be crushed into fiber. It takes three plastic bottles to create one pair of sneakers.

The shoes themselves are designed in Paris, with some models crafted from GOTS-certified cotton, grown in such a way that nutrients are returned to the soil. Although the brand does use Brazilian leather, tanned using vegetable dyes, one in every four Veja sneaker models is vegan.

Using a high proportion of environmentally friendly raw materials, purchased according to fair trade principles and produced in factories with high social standards, does have its price, however: The production cost of a pair of a Veja sneakers is five to seven times higher than a traditional sneaker. To help recoup this outlay, the brand eschews traditional marketing and advertising channels, which can account for up to 70% of the cost of any popular sneaker brand. Eliminating ads, brand ambassadors, and billboards allows Veja to price its sneakers competitively.

By establishing such a strong point of difference, the sneaker itself has become the brand's communication tool, through which it can talk to consumers about responsibility, transparency, and the ingredients of its sneakers. Veja also uses its retail stores to promote the brand's message and engage with consumers; the Veja store in New York's NoLita neighborhood was designed with limited waste materials and is powered by renewable wind energy by Abest. A video display of their manufacturing process greets customers on arrival, and the store will also feature lectures on social and environmental issues, events, and product launches.

DISCUSSION QUESTIONS:

1. What makes Veja sneakers sustainable?
2. What gives Veja sneakers their "the cool factor"?
3. Explain why Veja does not use traditional advertising and marketing channels to sell its sneakers.

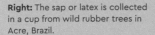

Right: The sap or latex is collected in a cup from wild rubber trees in Acre, Brazil.

Far right: Organic cotton is grown and purchased according to fair-trade principles.

Below: The finished product.

Part 4
Use/Care/Repair

CHAPTER 09: CONSUMPTION

The old joke "I have a closet full of clothes, but nothing to wear" is no longer acceptable given the state of the planet. Most consumers admit to having unused clothes or more clothes than needed in their closets. In fact, at the end of the 2010s, people were buying 400% more clothing on average than consumers did 20 years earlier.[106] And fashion consumption is still expected to grow. Purchasing more clothing than we actually need or wear is known as "overconsumption."

OVERCONSUMPTION

Overconsumption: *the state or an instance of consuming too much food, drink, fuel, clothing, etc.*

Collins Dictionary

Since the proliferation of advertising in the twentieth century, consumers have been programed to shop frequently for the latest trends and to satisfy their inner cravings through instant gratification. This has fostered an insatiable appetite to overconsume cheap and fashionable clothing, a root cause of all the pressing environmental issues the fashion industry faces. These buying habits are so deeply embedded in consumer behavior that it will take a significant commitment to replace them with a more socially responsible mindset. Both consumers and producers have a role to play in this shift.

CONSUMERS AS ACTIVISTS

However, the movement has begun and consumers are increasingly voting with their wallets against unsustainable

Money Fashion Power, Fashion Revolution's zine, explores the purchasing power of consumers.

brands. Attracted to purpose-driven brands that are building sustainability into their products, services, and entire supply chains, consumers are influenced by the words, values, and actions of a company and its leadership when they make their purchasing decisions.

Many consumers believe their individual protest actions, such as boycotting a company or speaking out on social media, can make a difference in how companies or even governments behave. No longer just buyers of goods and services, consumers are becoming active stakeholders who are investing their time and attention and want to feel a sense of shared purpose.

Consumer activism: *a term that describes a variety of disparate movements that seek to influence the behavior of companies through activities ranging from providing information to boycotts, pickets, and litigation, with the aim of forcing companies to act in a way that benefits the perceived interests of consumers.*

The SAGE Encyclopedia of Business Ethics and Society

Environmental issues have become very personal. If people can see ways in which they can take positive action individually, they will, and in doing so cause major disruptions to companies or industries that in turn cause structural shifts.

For instance, public anxiety and anger about single-use plastic fueled many consumers to look at their consumption behavior and to demand change, commitments, and action. Single-use plastics, or disposable plastics, are used only once before they are thrown away or recycled. Roughly 300 million tons of plastic is produced each year, with 50% of it for single-use purposes. Only 14% of plastic items are recycled.[107] The nature of petroleum-based disposable plastic makes it difficult to recycle because new virgin materials and chemicals must be added to do so. This is why a shift in consumption was so crucial.

The New Plastics Economy Global Commitment was formed as a collaboration with the United Nations in 2018 and is being led by the Ellen MacArthur Foundation (see page 27). The initiative consists of 250 organizations who are ultimately responsible for 20% of the plastic produced worldwide. A diverse group of members include H&M, Unilever, Kering, L'Oréal, Nestlé, and Coca-Cola.[108]

PLASTIC REVOLUTION

2017
China announces ban on 24 types of imported foreign waste from the US, UK, and EU

2018
David Attenborough's *Blue Planet II* raises the issue of plastics strewn across oceans worldwide

2018
California becomes the first US state to ban plastic straws in restaurants and aims to ban single use plastic by 2030

2018
European Parliament votes for complete ban on single use plastics by 2021

2019
India announces ban on six different types of single-use plastics by Mahatma Gandhi's birthday, October 2, 2022

Ultimately, the aim of the initiative is to promote a circular economy for plastic, to move from single-use to reusable models, keeping materials in use and out of the environment. Corporations joining the commitment will work to eliminate problematic or unnecessary single-use plastic, ensure all plastics can either be reused, recycled, or composted, and circulate everything they do use, to keep it in the economy and out of landfill. They aim to achieve this by 2025.[109]

Fashion brands are also taking steps toward circularity by using plastic from recycled water bottles instead of so-called virgin plastic. Everlane is among fashion brands trying to use less plastic or eliminate it altogether.

BRANDS AS ACTIVISTS

Today, a growing number of fashion companies are embracing the opportunity to promote their social and environmental credentials. Linking a brand's values or purpose to relevant issues that reflect the times is on the rise, as companies tap into people's desire for change. In this climate, doing good can become a competitive

Opposite: Everlane's Puffy Puffer, made from recycled plastic bottles, launched with a 38,000-person waitlist.

Left: Stella McCartney's 2020 Resort presentation, Milan 2019, referenced the climate protests sweeping the globe.

advantage, as it becomes a point of difference for consumers when they're making purchasing decisions.

Stella McCartney is renowned for her environmental activism. For her brand's Fall 2019 advertising campaign, the company teamed up with members of UK-based Extinction Rebellion, an international movement that uses non-violent civil disobedience to protest against unethical and damaging environmental practices. The activists modeled her range, which consisted of such materials as organic cotton, recycled polyester, and Econyl, regenerated nylon. Extinction Rebellion protesters had previously called for a cancellation of London Fashion Week in 2019 due to its impact on consumption and asked consumers to stop purchasing and take part in a year-long boycott on buying any new clothes.[110]

The advertising campaign promoted the brand's more environmentally conscious clothes, while also calling for climate action. A short film was released accompanying the campaign in which environmentalist Jane Goodall reads a poem by American novelist Jonathan Safran Foer.

There is a delicate balance when brands and activists work together, yet McCartney and XR activists hoped the campaign would be provocative, that it would get people talking about fashion and environmental issues.

SUSTAINABLE (AND CIRCULAR) CONSUMPTION

Enabling consumers to personally take steps toward sustainability as part of their brand experience is a powerful strategy for building loyalty and trust with that brand. It can be achieved only when companies choose to collaborate with customers expecting these changes, and scale their circular strategies alongside them. Truly sustainable companies are those that invite consumers to join each step of the redesign and innovation process through their marketing efforts.

From a consumer's perspective, sustainable consumption means making more conscious choices and in some cases buying less.

Germany's Grüner Knopf (Green Button), launched in 2019, is the world's first government-sponsored sustainability label designed to help improve issues in textile manufacturing. The Green Button sets requirements for both products and companies. Products must comply with 26 social and environmental requirements and companies are required to demonstrate human rights and environmental due diligence according to a set of 20 criteria based on the UN Guiding Principles on Business and Human Rights, as well as sector-specific recommendations made by the Organisation for Economic Co-operation and Development.[111]

The hope is that the Green Button, as a recognizable sign, will help consumers pay attention to sustainability when buying clothes and purchase more products that are produced ecologically and fairly.

PRINCIPLES OF SUSTAINABLE CONSUMPTION

As consumers, one of the best things we can do for the environment is to get more use out of clothing we already own, reducing our individual consumption habits. Consuming clothing in a sustainable manner includes shopping smarter, caring for and repairing clothing, and properly disposing of unwanted garments at the end of their use.

SMART SHOPPING

There are three key ways for consumers to make more informed purchases:

1. **Check labels:** The "made in" label of a garment generally indicates the fiber content of the clothing, country of origin, manufacturer/dealer identity, and care instructions. In terms of country of origin, a good rule to follow is "the closer to place of purchase the better."
2. **Check fabrics:** Some materials clearly have more impact on the environment than others (see pages 66–7). When buying new clothes, for instance, make a point of purchasing items made from organic cotton, lyocell, hemp, bamboo, or recycled materials (such as recycled plastic).
3. **Research brands:** Retailers and brands that invest in sustainability are transparent about the origins of the products they sell. Doing your part as a sustainable consumer means researching or asking brands about these origins.

Germany's state-approved "Green Button" label for environmentally certified textiles.

Consumers will buy organic, Fairtrade, and circular clothing more often if there is sufficient opportunity to compare brands and products in the full scope of features—from design and quality to environmental performance. Rank a Brand is an independent brand-comparison website that assesses and ranks consumer brands in several sectors on sustainability and social responsibility. Rank a Brand assigns a sustainability score to each brand so that consumers can make more responsible purchases.

CLOTHING CARE

By reducing the general maintenance of clothing and using alternative, energy-efficient means to care for it, the lifespan of clothes can be lengthened.

The following can help with garment care:

1. Reading the care label information on clothing.
2. Washing clothing less and at low temperatures (86° Farenheit/30° Celcius).
3. Using the dryer as little as possible and opting for an airier alternative.
4. Ironing a little less by putting freshly washed clothes on a hanger as quickly as possible to avoid wrinkles.

Stella McCartney garments contain a CleverCare logo as a reminder to consider the environment when washing clothes. CleverCare was developed in collaboration with Swiss global standard washcare label company Ginetex. CleverCare labels provide explicit care instructions designed to help customers get the most out of their clothing through proper care—which also leads to water and energy savings through less frequent machine-washing and drying—as well as guidance on ironing and professional laundering techniques.

Encouraging people to make the most of the clothes they already have, Love Your Clothes is part of the Sustainable Clothing Action Plan (SCAP), which is coordinated by the Waste & Resources Action Programme (WRAP), a not-for-profit organization that receives Government support across the United Kingdom. Launched in 2014, the campaign was developed to inspire consumers to buy sustainable clothing brands and extend the lifespan of their old garments by restyling them for a fresh look, doing a simple repair, or transforming them into something else entirely.

The type of fabric from which clothes are made is another consideration when it comes to the negative environmental impact of clothing care. Washing garments made from

Left: Love Your Clothes provides consumers with practical tips to make clothing last longer.

Right: CleverCare logo from Ginetex. CleverCare encourages consumers to get the most from their clothes by caring for them better.

synthetics such as polyester and acrylic release microfibers, tiny bits of plastic that detach from clothing and make their way into freshwater systems. Fashion Revolution estimates that one regular wash containing synthetic clothing releases as many as 700,000 fibers.[112] France is the first country to take legislative steps against microfiber pollution. As of 2025, all new washing machines in France must include a filter to stop the release of microfibers.[113]

WASH-LESS CLOTHING

A new wave of clothing brands are designing garments that require less washing. How often people wash their clothes has historically been tied to good hygiene and even social class. Washing machines account for 17% of home water usage in the United States and 25% of the carbon footprint of a garment comes from clothing care.[114]

Unbound Merino creates wool travel clothes that can go weeks without being washed, while Wool & Prince designs Oxford shirts, T-shirts, and boxer briefs using merino wool. Wool is naturally breathable and temperature regulating with moisture wicking properties. It is also resistant to odor and dirt and ideal, therefore, for infrequent laundering. Pangaia creates seaweed fiber and certified-organic cotton T-shirts treated with peppermint oil to keep the shirts fresher longer.

CLOTHING REPAIR

Learning to mend clothing can be a very useful skill. DIY sewing and knitting workshops offer help to consumers as they navigate their way into the world of repairing. In 2009, Martine Postma, a Dutch journalist, ran an experiment in Amsterdam in which she invited a group of friends to a "repair café," a free event where people could bring in broken items and work together with volunteers to try and fix them. Following the great success of this experiment, Postma set up the Repair Café Foundation. Today, according to the Foundation, 2,000 repair cafés operate in local communities in over 35 countries.[115]

Fashion brands offering free clothing repairs are also on the rise. Patagonia's Worn Wear program features pop-up events where customers can bring in used clothing items for repair

(see page 150). Similarly, Taylor Stitch, San Francisco's classic menswear brand, cleans and repairs its used products and then sells them on its online platform, Restitch, at a discounted rate. Both Patagonia and Taylor Stitch partner with Yerdle, a company that builds and operates clothing refurbishment and resale programs for brands.

CONSUMERS AS CO-CREATORS

A co-creation design process is carried out, fully or partly, in collaboration with future users. Creating a sense of ownership of a product means a user is less willing to part with it. This means putting the user at the start of the process, rather than considering them merely as the recipient at the end—making the user journey more circular.

The process also presents a valuable opportunity for brands to engage directly with consumers, building stronger trust than ever before by ensuring they play an integral role in their sustainability efforts in a sharing economy.

Sharing Economy: an economic system that is based on people sharing possessions and services, either for free or for payment, usually using the internet to organize this.
Cambridge Dictionary

Innovation is coming from smaller fashion brands as they explore circularity by digitizing the process of making clothes and accessories by co-creating with consumers. Solve, a Romanian-Danish innovation studio focused on design and sustainability, launched a downloadable collection of handbag patterns known as S-bags, which co-creators can use to make items from pre-owned materials from home. The S-bags can be made at a nearby makerspace, a communal space containing a variety of tools and machines such as laser cutters and 3D printers. The perceived value of co-creation is that, by being involved in its creation, a consumer is encouraged to form a greater attachment to the product, making them more likely to use it for longer.

Preloved Taylor Stitch garments are
repaired and given new life on
Taylor Stitch's Restitch platform.

CONSUMERS AS USERS

Among younger consumers, there is a shift in attitude toward more access to goods and services and away from ownership. According to the World Economic Forum, the sharing economy will only grow in the immediate future as consumers become more comfortable with renting and leasing goods and services for a short period of time instead of buying them outright. While fashion rental companies already exist, the concept is likely to evolve to more subscription and brand-based models (see pages 113–5).

Founded in Amsterdam in 2014, LENA the Fashion Library is a store and web-shop in which customers can borrow secondhand and vintage clothes whenever they like, just like a normal library. To use the service, subscribers pay a fee for which they receive points they can use to borrow clothing.

For consumers who desire frequent style changes, borrowing clothing through subscription models is an attractive alternative to purchasing trendy fashions.

CONSUMERS AS LOCAL CITIZENS

Operating outside of the traditional fashion system enables independent designers or established fashion brands to build shorter supply chains by keeping design and production local. This home-grown approach brings with it a number of advantages.

1. **Builds local economy:** When consumers buy locally made clothing, significantly more of the money stays in the community, creating jobs and further strengthening the economic base of the whole community.

137

Downloadable S-bag from Solve
Design Studio, Denmark.

Flagship LENA the Fashion Library,
Westerstraat, Amsterdam.

2. **Connects consumers with people behind products:**
   When a consumer personally knows the people behind the
   business where they are buying local products and
   services, they enjoy a connection they would not
   otherwise have.
3. **Ensures better quality control:** The country in which a
   garment was made also tends to be an indicator of its
   quality. For instance, a garment that has not been
   shipped halfway around the world is more likely to be in
   much better condition when it arrives on a retailer's shelf.
4. **Reduces the carbon footprint:** Overall, clothing will
   travel far less throughout the supply chain, making
   logistics cleaner by significantly reducing any
   environmental impact.
5. **Generates less waste:** Eliminating unnecessary

transportation and delivery also means reducing the
amount of packaging being used.

The US outdoor brand The North Face and Fibershed
Backyard Project was one of the first bioregional garment
projects to be brought to market by a major brand. Launched
in 2014, the project aligns with the ethos of working with
what you have in your own backyard, and was about creating
as much of the garment as physically possible within 150
miles (240 km) of The North Face headquarters in Alameda,
California.

*Bioregion: a region defined by
characteristics of the natural environment
rather than by man-made divisions.* Lexico

Garments from The North Face's
Backyard Project, which connects
consumers to local producers
and products.

The project directly supported local fiber farmers. The growing
of the organic cotton took place regionally, but the carding,
spinning, and knitting was done in North and South Carolina
because there were no mills in the northern California region
which could do this type of work with the organic fibers.
While this may seem quite a distance, most materials travel
thousands of miles before making their way to the design
studios of fashion brands and the closets of consumers.

THINK PIECE:
**What benefits would drive consumers to shift
from owning their clothing to renting it?**

DIGITAL CONSUMPTION

The myriad ways we consume fashion has been radically
transformed by the digitization of daily life. Many people
believe that the instant gratification of "see now, buy now"
apps like Instagram are damaging to both the industry and
the planet because they support a throwaway fashion
culture. However, through the internet and social media the
majority of consumers also have greater access to more
information about the environmental impact of their clothing
choices, which can ultimately lead to more mindful and
meaningful consumption.

CIRCULAR LEADERS:
SUZANNE SMULDERS, ANGELA JANSEN,
DIANA JANSEN, AND ELISA JANSEN

Sisters Angela, Diana, and Elisa Jansen began selling secondhand clothes on their online store, Doortje Originals, in 2006, becoming the first vintage web-shop in the Netherlands. They soon recognized, however, that people wear secondhand clothes a few times only. Teaming up with their friend Suzanne Smulders, they developed the idea of a closet a user can borrow from whenever they feel like having something new. LENA the Fashion Library was launched in Amsterdam in 2014, their venture helped by the fact that all four women had a background in the fashion and design industries.

With a shared passion, each woman has a unique role in the shop. Diana is a fashion designer and a buyer who curates the clothing collections, Angela creates the visual presence and imagery, Elisa is the business and people manager, while Suzanne specializes in communication and public relations.

In the future they wish to see an industry-wide shift from "ownership" to shared access, and for borrowing to become the norm for all.

(lena-library.com)

CHAPTER 10: TOOLS, ASSESSMENTS, AND STANDARDS

Consumers make choices every day in what they buy and who they buy it from. Increasingly they want to buy from companies that align with their own values: socially responsible, people-friendly companies that create products in safe, healthy environments. Companies use assessment tools and certifications as a means of measuring and validating the environmental sustainability of their products—information that can be communicated to their customers.

CIRCULAR CRITERIA

Circular brands are careful stewards of the planet by minimizing their environmental footprints. They can provide certified or verifiable details about how and under what conditions their products are made. Leading the way are brands taking steps by using organic cotton and eco-friendly materials, reducing energy or water consumption, or eliminating toxic chemicals in production. They are setting targets and informing their customers of progress made along the way.

An assessment scoring tool provides a framework to measure the environmental sustainability impacts of materials in the product development cycle. It assists companies in understanding and predicting the impact of their business decisions.

Certifications from various independent organizations focus on establishing and enforcing environmental standards. Companies can include these certifications on a label, packaging, or in store to provide a seal of approval as proof and validation for their sustainability efforts.

B CORPORATIONS

A "B Corporation" (B Corp) is a business with a certification awarded by the non-profit B Lab that meets rigorous assessment standards of social and environmental performance, accountability, and transparency.[116] In order to be recognized as a B Corp, a company needs to pass an 80-point assessment, but it also has to adopt a legal framework that explicitly says it will account for all of its stakeholders when making decisions.[117]

B Corporation: a certification for businesses that balances profits with a positive social and environmental performance.
Macmillan Dictionary

Outdoor clothing retailer Patagonia registered as one of the first B Corp fashion companies in 2012. Today, there are over 3,000 Certified B Corps in more than 70 countries and 150 industries worldwide.[118]

Patagonia works to create stronger
communities and a healthier
environment.

PRODUCT LIFE CYCLE

Fashion brands striving for higher social and environmental
standards, and certifications such as B Corp, may conduct a
Life Cycle Assessment (LCA) of their products and processes.

A product's life cycle refers to all the stages from its raw
material through to the product's introduction in the
marketplace and its exit. All stages of a product's life
cycle have an impact on the environment, and can lead to
issues such as climate change, water toxicity, and natural
resource depletion.

LIFE CYCLE ASSESSMENT

Life Cycle Assessment is a tool to measure the
environmental impact of products from their inception to the
end of their use. This means all phases of a product are
considered and analyzed, from raw materials to production,
packaging, transport, retail, consumer use, disposal, or
recycling.

Before deciding to use an LCA, a brand must determine what
they want to achieve from the assessment, along with the
life cycle stage(s) and type of impacts they want to review.

A fiber, a design, or a process are all factors that can be used to indicate how, and to what extent, a garment's lifespan harms the environment.

Many brands use LCAs to assess products from "Cradle to Grave"—that is, from raw material to final disposal. Some may also assess from "Cradle to Gate," meaning raw material to factory. Then there is the circular approach, "Cradle to Cradle," which assesses raw material to recycling point, as opposed to final disposal.

There are many methodologies and tools that brands can employ to perform an LCA. These can also be used to make comparisons between different products, to measure which has the lowest environmental impact. By performing even a simple LCA, a brand can get to know its products better.

LIFE CYCLE ASSESSMENT METHODS
The LCA research methodology used by B Lab to gain insight into the full life cycle of the products of a company under consideration for B Corp certification are done by:

- Compiling an inventory of energy and material inputs and environmental outputs.
- Evaluating the potential environmental impacts associated with identified inputs and outputs.
- Interpreting the results to help make a more informed decision about the human health and environmental impacts of products, processes, and activities.

BENEFITS OF LIFE CYCLE ASSESSMENT
Life Cycle Assessments can play a significant role in providing critical information on how to improve a fashion brand's sustainability challenges. Benefits of an LCA include the following:

- **Identifying environmental impacts:** LCA results can indicate early in the development process if there is a real potential for sustainability and can lead to further innovation. Companies may introduce or re-evaluate sustainability initiatives, programs, and processes.
- **Product design and process improvements:** LCA can promote responsible design and redesign of products and

THE FOUR MAIN STEPS IN THE LCA PROCESS:			
1. GOAL AND SCOPE	**2. LIFE CYCLE INVENTORY**	**3. LIFE CYCLE IMPACT**	**4. INTERPRETATION**
Determines the intended application (goal), which processes are environmental concerns, and any economic or social good provided by the product or service in question (scope).	Examines a model of environmental inputs and outputs associated with a product or service, such as the use of raw materials and energy, the emission of pollutants, and the waste streams.	Classifies the data according to environmental impacts, evaluates these impacts by what is most important, and translates them into themes such as global climate change, natural resources, pollution, and human health.	Analyzes the impact assessment data, which leads to the conclusion of whether the ambitions from the goal and scope can be met. Ensures conclusions and recommendations are well-substantiated.

Adidas Alphabounce + Parley sports apparel made from recycled ocean plastic waste. Adidas conducts life cycle assessments to learn about the environmental impacts of its products.

processes leading to reduced overall environmental impacts and the reduced use and release of toxic materials.[119]

- **Customer and stakeholder engagement:** A company may also communicate the results to their customers and the industry, which can suggest areas for improvement or strengthen the market position of a new product.

MISTRA FUTURE FASHION: A LIFE CYCLE ASSESSMENT EXAMPLE

Mistra Future Fashion is a research program focusing on the circular economy, which delivers insight and solutions used by the Swedish Fashion Industry and other stakeholders to significantly improve their environmental performance and strengthen their global competitiveness.

A Life Cycle Assessment by Mistra Future Fashion was used to evaluate the environmental impact of six garments—a T-shirt, a pair of jeans, a dress, a jacket, a pair of socks, and a hospital uniform—using indicators of carbon footprint, energy use,

water scarcity, the impact of land use on soil quality, freshwater use, eco-toxicity, and human toxicity. The environmental impact of the six garments was then scaled up to represent Swedish national clothing consumption over one year.

The chart below summarizes the results for two of the indicators, carbon footprint and energy use, at the level of total clothing purchases and uses in Sweden over one year.

Interpretation of the LCA results found that 80% of the climate impact of Swedish clothing

THE CLIMATE IMPACT OF SWEDISH CLOTHING CONSUMPTION

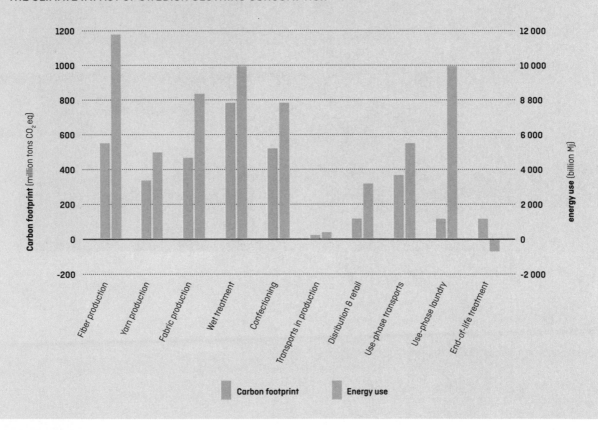

consumption stems from the production phase. This means most of the environmental impact happens before the garments are on the retail floor or in the hands of the consumer.

Lastly, the Mistra Future Fashion LCA report concluded that both producers and consumers can help reduce the climate impact of clothing consumption. Producers can begin with technical production improvements and users can make behavioral changes such as consuming less, or recycling.[120]

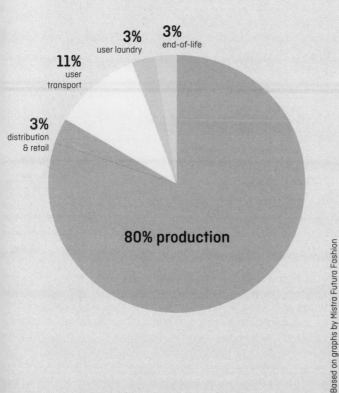

3% user laundry

3% end-of-life

11% user transport

3% distribution & retail

80% production

Based on graphs by Mistra Futura Fashion

THE HIGG INDEX

The Higg Index is a suite of sustainability assessment tools used by the Sustainable Apparel Coalition (SAC) to assess the manufacturing facility, brand, and product impacts of textile production. The Higg Index assessment toolkit consists of product tools, facility tools, and brand and retail tools:

1. **Product tools:** These can be used during the product's design and completion phases to predict environmental impacts.
2. **Facility tools:** These measure impacts at individual factories by conducting assessments that are then verified by SAC-approved, on-site assessors.
3. **Brand and retail tools:** These measure the environmental impacts of a brand or retailer's operations.

The SAC has more than 200 members who use the Higg Index tool suite for measuring sustainability. Members include some of the world's biggest brands, such as Adidas, Disney, Gap, Levi's®, Nike, and Target.[121]

CRADLE TO CRADLE CERTIFICATION

Cradle to Cradle Certified™ is a globally recognized measure of safer, more sustainable products specifically made for the circular economy. Cradle to Cradle (C2C) certification ensures that products remain in a continuous circle, where there is no waste. To receive certification, a product is assessed on the C2C design principles that provide guidance in five key categories:

1. Material health is knowing the chemicals and materials in a product and working toward making them safe.
2. Material utilization means a product is intentionally designed to be safely returned to nature or industry for its next use.
3. Renewable energy and climate management means working toward a future where manufacturing is powered by clean energy and makes a positive impact.
4. Water stewardship is managing and protecting water as a precious and shared resource for all.

C2C Certified™ jeans from C&A
Europe. C&A was the first retailer
to launch Gold Level C2C
Certified™ T-shirts.

5. Social fairness upholds human rights and responsible business practices for all people.

The C2C Products Program is based on the concept of continuous improvement and thus there are five possible levels of achievement within each of the standard's five key requirement categories:

- **Basic:** environmental risks are assessed and a policy is put into place.
- **Bronze:** a strategy is developed at the final manufacturing stages.

- **Silver:** management systems are in place and environmental data is collected and analyzed.
- **Gold:** responsible sourcing management systems are in place.
- **Platinum:** environmental objectives are fully incorporated, achieving the company's goals.

To reach a desired achievement level within each category, the product must meet all of the requirements for that level, in addition to the requirements at all lower levels.[122] In 2017, C&A, the international Dutch clothing store chain, became the first retailer to launch a line of Gold Level C2C Certified™

T-shirts. The T-shirts are reasonably priced and made entirely from biocotton, including the labels and stitching that are made traditionally from nylon or polyester. Colors and prints were created in collaboration with chemical companies that helped create non-toxic coloring dyes. If discarded on a compost heap, the T-shirt will break down within 11 weeks.

CRADLE TO CRADLE AND FASHION CIRCULARITY

The Fashion Positive Initiative developed by C2C works with a community of brands, such as Stella McCartney and Mara Hoffman, to reduce waste and produce clothes safely, fairly, and efficiently. C2C Certified™ is the only standard of its kind to ensure that all materials created have a pathway for reuse or compostability.

A C2C approach to product design means that organic cotton farmers can grow their crops without toxic fertilizers and pesticides, and those involved in the production processes are not exposed to harmful chemicals because none are used. In addition, by using renewable energy, offsetting carbon emissions, and keeping the water clean in the production process, C2C Certified™ products support both the health of ecosystems and the communities in which they are manufactured.

> **THINK PIECE:**
> Why is it important for a brand to embrace life cycle assessments? Do you think a value retailer like C&A can become more sustainable and maintain profitability if it conducts an LCA and follows its recommendations?

CIRCULAR LEADER: YVON CHOUINARD

Yvon Chouinard is an American environmentalist, mountain climber, surfer, fisherman, and author. He founded Patagonia in 1973 out of his small blacksmith shop in Ventura, California, where he developed hardware gear and then clothing for mountaineers and climbers. He became committed to environmentalism after witnessing horrible land degradation at the hands of developers during a climbing trip to Southern Argentina in the 1980s.

Given this environmental focus, Patagonia strives to make clothing as responsibly as possible so that their creation causes no unnecessary harm. In 2012 it became the first Californian business to become a B Corp, adopting the stringent standards relating to labor practices and social and environmental impacts. Furthermore, Chouinard has promised to make Patagonia carbon neutral by 2025.

The company is also dedicated to product quality and durability, recognizing that as the life cycle of their products increases, the carbon footprint decreases.

Chouinard believes that he makes money every time he makes a decision that is best for the planet, and Patagonia's success proves that it is possible to run a highly profitable, successful business by eschewing fast fashion. Over the years Patagonia, which is still family owned, has become a billion-dollar global brand, making it the ultimate do-good-and-do-well company.

(patagonia.com)

CASE STUDY #4: USE/CARE/REPAIR

PATAGONIA: THE REPAIR WAGON

Patagonia is an American outdoor gear and clothing brand, founded in 1973 by climber Yvon Chouinard, which advocates environmental stewardship. Since its inception the brand has adopted sustainable practices, including using organic and recycled materials and encouraging customers not to buy new products but instead to care for the ones they already own. The Worn Wear program is an important part of this ethos.

HISTORY OF PATAGONIA'S WORN WEAR PROGRAM

2013 The Worn Wear film and blog are launched to celebrate "The Stories We Wear."

2014 A repair wagon is built by artist/surfer Jay Nelson out of reclaimed redwood wine barrels and runs on biodiesel.

2015 Patagonia kicks off the first Worn Wear mobile repair tour across America. As of 2019, the Worn Wear team has done 12 additional tours around North America.

2016 Europe kicks off first Worn Wear tour, making 50 stops in five countries.

2017 Launch of www.wornwear.com.

2018 South America kicks off first Worn Wear tour.

2019 Japan kicks off first Worn Wear tour.

What does a Worn Wear event look like? A crew of repair techs and brand ambassadors begin spreading the word on social media, encouraging customers to bring their worn, damaged clothing to be mended. Next, Patagonia's biodiesel repair wagon nicknamed "Delia" (pictured opposite) hits the road. The event takes place where the wagon is parked. With a self-contained power system, Delia runs sewing machines off the grid and provides a treasure trove of zippers, buttons, threads, and patches. The event offers free clothing repairs on any brand, DIY repair tips, and, on occasion, deals on used Patagonia gear. The repair mission stops at college campuses, retail shops, eco events, farms, and festivals to keep what consumers already own in use and out of landfills.

Alongside its commitment to circularity and product longevity, Patagonia has become a leader in clothing repair. Since the Worn Wear tours began in 2015, Patagonia has increased the number of employees at their repair facility from 35 to 84 and added a second shift to keep up with the demand. The Patagonia garment repair facility is the largest of its kind in North America, completing about 50,000 repairs per year.[123] The company has also teamed up with iFixit, an online repair manual, to create repair guides so customers can easily make repairs themselves. The Worn Wear platform was so successful that a permanent online website was launched—www.wornwear.com—where customers can buy secondhand Patagonia goods and trade in Patagonia items they are no longer using for credit in Patagonia retail stores, on Patagonia.com, or wornwear.com.

DISCUSSION QUESTIONS:

1. How does Patagonia's repair options encourage their customers to buy fewer clothes?
2. What makes the Worn Wear tours so successful?
3. In what ways can clothing repair help consumers become more environmentally responsible?

Freitag offers some 4,500 unique products.

Part 5
Renew

CHAPTER 11: END OF USE

Waste occurs all along the fashion supply chain and throughout consumer use, right up to garment disposal. Becoming a responsible participant in the fashion industry, whether as a producer or consumer, means producing less waste. Conserving resources is ideal but what happens when a piece of clothing is no longer wanted?

WASTE NOT, WANT NOT

Even though new circularity models extend the life cycle of clothing, it still often ends up being incinerated or in landfills.

INCINERATION

Many brands have been known to burn their unwanted clothing to maintain the exclusivity of their brand image. The destruction of excess inventory is intended to stop products from being stolen or sold at discounted prices.

In 2017, the luxury brand Burberry incinerated 37.8 million dollars' worth of unwanted clothing and cosmetics. There was much public criticism, which renewed scrutiny over such a wasteful practice, and Burberry quickly pledged to stop destroying their unwanted or excess products.[124]

LANDFILLS

Since the Industrial Revolution, out-of-date, unwanted materials have been disposed of in waste dumps, known as landfills.

Landfill: *disposal of waste material by burying it under layers of earth.*
Collins Dictionary

Galeries Lafayette, Paris, France, the only country that has implemented EPR legislation on textile producers. The Galeries Lafayette Group has its own sustainable development strategy, Go For Good.

Today, decades' worth of discarded garments lie forgotten in such sites. As these clothing and textiles decompose they release methane, a harmful greenhouse gas that is a significant contributor to climate change (see page 77). Chemicals and dyes can also leak into the soil and water, causing contamination and harming humans and wildlife.[125]

In a circular economy, landfills would be temporary storage places for waste awaiting further processing or treatment, rather than the permanent solution. A process called enhanced landfill mining aims to reclaim the value of discarded waste materials by salvaging these materials from landfills. By recovering these resources and selling them back into the market, this system can reintroduce old waste into new material cycles, creating a fully closed-loop system.[126]

There are many alternatives to extend the life of clothing past its intended use. As collective awareness of the negative impacts of the linear system grows, more consumers are seeking solutions to reusing and disposing of unwanted clothing. In other words, how we "unmake" clothing matters—and it's just as important as how we make clothing.

EXTENDED PRODUCER RESPONSIBILITY (EPR)

As waste piles up, governments are increasingly holding producers accountable for the waste they produce. Extended Producer Responsibility (EPR) is a policy approach where producers are given responsibility—be it financial and/or physical—for the entire life cycle of the products they produce and sell in the market, with a particular focus on end-of-product-life management. Assigning such responsibility provides incentives to prevent waste at its source, promote eco-design, and support the achievement of public recycling.

France is currently the only country that has imposed a mandatory EPR on textile producers. Since 2007, French companies that produce and import clothing, linen, and footwear are responsible by law to directly manage the collection, reuse, and recycling of their products.[127]

TAKE-BACK PROGRAMS

A take-back program collects used clothing and textiles at a retailer's point of sale and gives them a new life through reuse or recycling (see pages 112–113). A company may implement

WHERE DOES UNWANTED CLOTHING GO?

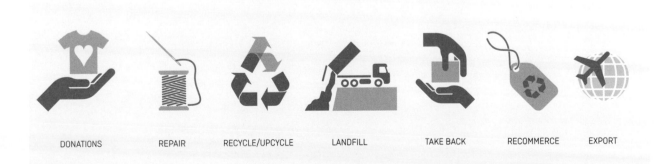

DONATIONS · REPAIR · RECYCLE/UPCYCLE · LANDFILL · TAKE BACK · RECOMMERCE · EXPORT

a take-back program in collaboration with material processing firms or through internal end-of-use logistics.

The vast majority of clothing brands are not yet required by any legislation to provide for the end-of-life recovery of their products. Retailers may take responsibility for the social and environmental cost of producing their clothes by establishing clothing collection bins in their stores, but what happens to those items after they are collected? Responsible retailers will ensure proper recycling or disposal methods are in place once collection bins are filled. A retailer may hire a materials processing firm to organize the transportation, sorting, and transfer of the clothing for reuse. I:CO, for instance, is a Swiss company that collects discarded clothing, shoes, belts, and bags from collection points in the United States and Europe, working with approximately 60 retailers, including The North Face, Levi's®, and H&M. The collected clothing is transported to the sorting and recycling plant and is then processed so that it can be resold as secondhand or recycled.

For a retailer, there are multiple benefits for implementing a take-back program:

- Sustainable end-of-use solution.
- Reducing the environmental impact of textile waste and saving resources.
- Enabling unwanted clothing to be reprocessed, avoiding material waste streams.
- Engaging customers in a retailer's sustainability initiative.
- Encouraging customers to use clothing more sustainably.

Consumer incentives, such as coupons and gift cards, that encourage take-back donations have been relatively successful in diverting textiles from landfills. Knickey, an organic cotton underwear start-up, offers free shipping labels and a pair of undergarments to customers who send the brand their unwanted underwear, bras, socks, and tights. The brand works with an industrial recycler who shreds the collected items and downcycles the materials into insulation.

Reet Aus's Up-shirts, made with recycled pre-consumer textile waste, are bestsellers in Estonia.

Downcycle: *to create an object or material of lesser value from a discarded object or material of higher value.*
Merriam-Webster Dictionary

There is debate that these incentives and rewards ultimately increase new clothing consumption, thereby generating further waste streams. However, most brands agree that some incentive is necessary to encourage consumers to bring their unwanted clothes back to stores, rather than simply throwing them away.

RECYCLING

A closed-loop recycling process means the retailer or manufacturer has an end-of-use process in place and reuses the collected items for products within their organization. An open-loop recycling process ensures the clothing and textiles are collected, sorted, and processed, ultimately to be reused in various industries.

COLLECTION AND SORTING

Post-consumer clothing donations are generally picked up from large containers or pop-up collection bins placed in public

A CIRCULAR TAKE-BACK PROGRAM

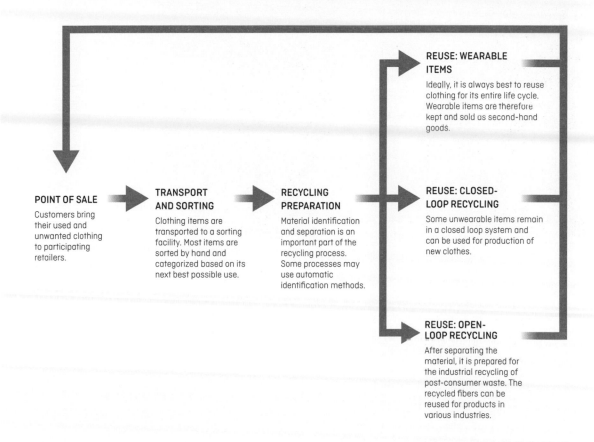

POINT OF SALE

Customers bring their used and unwanted clothing to participating retailers.

TRANSPORT AND SORTING

Clothing items are transported to a sorting facility. Most items are sorted by hand and categorized based on its next best possible use.

RECYCLING PREPARATION

Material identification and separation is an important part of the recycling process. Some processes may use automatic identification methods.

REUSE: WEARABLE ITEMS

Ideally, it is always best to reuse clothing for its entire life cycle. Wearable items are therefore kept and sold as second-hand goods.

REUSE: CLOSED-LOOP RECYCLING

Some unwearable items remain in a closed loop system and can be used for production of new clothes.

REUSE: OPEN-LOOP RECYCLING

After separating the material, it is prepared for the industrial recycling of post-consumer waste. The recycled fibers can be reused for products in various industries.

places. Bins are typically placed strategically in high traffic, high visibility areas such as retail stores, parking lots in business centers, and shopping malls to help maximize donations.

Once collected, clothing is identified as either wearable or unwearable. Wearable items can be donated to charitable organizations or designated for resale. The items that are no longer wearable are sent to processing facilities.

PROCESSING

Sorting and recycling are easy when clothes are made of one fiber. Unfortunately, most garments produced today consist of a blend of synthetic polyester and cotton, which influences the method of recycling and durability. Manual sorting processes increase the price for recycled textiles, making it difficult to compete with raw (virgin) materials.

Left and right: RAEMADE designs from Christopher Raeburn's Spring/Summer 2020 collection, New Horizons. Raeburn no longer presents catwalk shows because of the waste they create.

For natural textiles, such as cotton and wool, incoming items are sorted in terms of color and material. The clothing is then mechanically stripped and shredded into smaller fibers and combined with other chosen fibers, depending on the planned end-use of the recycled fiber.

The recycling process works somewhat differently for polyester-based materials. The first stage is to remove zippers and buttons and then to cut the clothing into smaller pieces. The smaller pieces are then crushed into finer particles, melted, and spun into new fibers.

Lastly, because the recycling process stretches and weakens fibers, only a small percentage of recycled clothes are used to create new textiles. Developing the technology to maximize the value of recovered materials and a market for recycled fibers is a key challenge in the move to bring a circular fashion system to scale.

FABSCRAP, a non-profit textile recycling program in New York, lets brands send their unwanted textiles to their warehouse, thereby diverting them from landfills. Since 2017, the company's team of "trash nerds" have collected over 230,000 pounds (104,300 kg) of commercial textile waste.[128] FABSCRAP reserves the best quality scraps for resale at its retail store and downcycles the smaller scraps.

UPCYCLING

Upcycling makes use of existing garments, using either pre-consumer or post-consumer waste or a combination of the two.

> *Upcycle: reuse discarded objects or material in such a way as to create a product of higher quality or value than the original.*
> Oxford Dictionary

Using existing fabric is one of the most environmentally friendly ways to produce clothes. While upcycling is usually associated with artisanal or craft designers with a homespun aesthetic, creative ideas and technology are bringing this design methodology to scale.

WASTE NO MORE

Waste No More was an exhibition about the reality of society's discarded clothing which also demonstrated the inherent aesthetics of recovered materials in contemporary design. Developed by sustainable clothing brand Eileen Fisher, unwanted clothing was transformed into artworks that reminded consumers of the importance of a circular fashion economy.

The exhibition asked viewers to reflect on the waste consumers create, and to be inspired by a "less is more" philosophy.

(wastenomore.com)

Eileen Fisher Waste No More launch and store event, Brooklyn, New York, 2019.

UPMADE® garments are upcycled from nontoxic production leftovers.

British designer Christopher Raeburn is a leading advocate of sustainability, synonymous with his brand's "remade, reduced, recycled" ethos. His fashion house creates distinctive and functional clothing and accessories from fabrics sourced from items such as unwanted garments, vintage military parachutes, life rafts, and silk maps from the 1950s.

Upcycling can also mean taking something of little or no value, such as production waste, and redesigning it to add value. Estonian fashion designer Reet Aus is dedicated to slow and ethical fashion. Her upcycled collection is entirely made from production leftovers. Using a circular model, the leftover materials are put back into production inside the same factory. Most mass-production manufacturers are left with an average 18% of pre-consumer textile waste that is usually taken to landfills or burned. Each garment in Reet Aus's collection is upcycled following UPMADE® certification criteria and saves on average 75% of water and 88% of energy.[129]

UPMADE®

UPMADE® is a technology which enables brands to upcycle on an industrial scale and obtain certification. Excess materials are turned into garments and waste is, therefore, brought back into the consumption chain.

Using the design, fabric, and production information from a brand's order, a waste analysis is conducted to determine what type of leftover materials will become available. Next, an environmental analysis is conducted to determine what resources can be saved as a result of upcycling.

Using specific production data, a new upcycled product is designed, leading to a physical sample. Each sample is presented alongside the results of a life cycle assessment that details how much energy and water it saves and how much CO_2 emission and waste it avoids. An order can then be placed, and the upcycled product put into production.

EXPORT

When faced with overflowing wardrobes, many people donate their used clothing to a charity. Although donating clothing may extend the lifespan of a garment, many consumers may not realize that when they donate unwanted clothing to charity shops, the majority of the clothing will be shipped to foreign markets. Donated garments deemed wearable may be resold, but the vast majority of items are wrapped into enormous plastic bundles and sent overseas. Developed economies such as the United States, United Kingdom, and European countries are the dominant suppliers of used clothing to the world.

Most of the world's used clothing exports end up being sold in developing countries, particularly the least developed ones.[130] Pakistan is currently the biggest importer of used clothes with 11% of the market, followed by Malaysia with 7.1%, according to M.I.T.'s Observatory of Economic Complexity.[131]

Trade policies regulating the used clothing trade often raise controversies. The influx of secondhand clothing has created employment, but the used clothing trade in many countries has displaced local garment manufacturing bases and suppressed the revival or future development of domestic industries.

> **THINK PIECE:**
> The majority of unprecedented growth in textile waste is driven by fast fashion and consumer behavior. In what ways can you properly dispose of your unwanted clothing?

CIRCULAR LEADER: CHRISTOPHER RAEBURN

Christopher Raeburn is the founder and creative director of Raeburn, a responsible design company based in the UK. A graduate of the prestigious Royal College of Art, he began his career as a freelance pattern cutter before setting up his own studio. He launched his first capsule collection, a range of reversible garments, at London Design Week in 2008, and in 2016 was named breakthrough designer of the year at the GQ Men of The Year awards.

Raeburn approaches his work from a design-led perspective, combining good design with sustainable production practices, ensuring that garments are fully recycled and recyclable. In 2017 he collaborated with the luxury goods brand MCM to create a capsule collection in which he deconstructed and reconstructed MCM's existing bags in his signature remade aesthetic.

He continues to be an outspoken critic of mindless mass consumption, even refusing to sell his garments during the Black Friday sales by disabling his online store.

The Raeburn Lab in East London is used not only as a making atelier, but also as a creative community hub that hosts workshops and tours to help inspire others.

(raeburndesign.co.uk)

CHAPTER 12: COLLABORATION AND INNOVATION

For many of us, fashion is a fundamental part of who we are, who we want to be, and how we perceive the world. Yet, at the same time, we know that for fashion to be circular and sustainable, it needs a fundamental redesign.

The fashion industry is expected to be worth around $3.3 trillion (£2.5 trillion) by the year 2030.[132] According to the United Nations, if we have not made significant changes to our environmental footprint by then, we can expect to experience serious global climate-related disasters in the 2040s.

A strong ecosystem of collaboration and innovation among everyone is urgently needed to tackle the obstacles ahead and to accelerate the fashion industry's transition to a circular system. A new generation of fashion creators and innovators are shaping the planet's future by utilizing new technologies and circular models to create products that can be recycled or re-engineered into new designs with minimal use of virgin materials, water, energy, and chemicals.

COLLABORATION

Collaboration is important in a circular fashion economy because everyone within and outside of the supply chain is interdependent upon each other and can benefit more from streamlined partnerships with a common objective. An industry shift from linear thinking to an understanding of the bigger picture and looking at the connections, not just the parts, for insight and solutions, is at the heart of circularity. Cooperation, reciprocity, transparency, and trust are important success factors if fashion is truly to become circular. Businesses, governments, educators, and consumers need to join forces.

BUSINESS

Circularity at scale can move forward only if large companies start working together to form new creative economies and share solutions. Innovative approaches, such as industrial symbiosis, bring companies into partnership to find ways to use the waste from one as raw materials for another.[133] For instance, company X exchanges waste streams with company Y, who then uses those waste streams in its own processes.

> *Industrial symbiosis is the mutually beneficial exchange of waste and by-products between three or more parties.*
> Circular Economy Practitioner Guide

Transparency is seen as openness, and it is only through transparent practices that a company can learn, can share relevant data and information, and compare efforts toward a common objective. Many brands have come together through the Ellen MacArthur Foundation's Make Fashion Circular initiative whose aim is "to ensure clothes are made from safe and renewable materials, new business models

The Copenhagen Fashion Summit, shown here in 2019, focuses on sustainability issues in fashion.

increase their use, and old clothes are turned into new."[134] When brands communicate with each other and share past experiences, trust increases as they work collectively.

GOVERNMENT

Collaborative efforts from leadership in both the public and private sectors, backed by actions at scale, are critical. Government and policymakers need to create a blueprint for change by enforcing brands to comply with higher standards. Investors need to support circular brands and the media must continue to raise awareness of the problems in the industry.

President Emmanuel Macron of France and François-Henri Pinault, CEO of Kering, launched the Fashion Pact in 2019. It consists of global fashion and textile companies with a shared set of objectives to reduce environmental impacts. The Fashion Pact has committed to achieving science-based targets in order to achieve zero greenhouse gas emissions by 2050, to keep global warming below 2.7° Fahrenheit (1.5° Celsius) until 2100, to restore natural ecosystems and protect species, and to reduce the use of single-use plastics to preserve aquatic life and the oceans.

CONSUMERS/USERS

While many consumers are still unaware of the environmental costs of the fashion industry, an increasing number believe their individual protest actions, such as boycotting a company or speaking out on social media, can make a difference in how companies or even governments behave. No longer just buyers of goods and services, consumers are active stakeholders who are investing their time and attention and want to feel a sense of purpose.

EDUCATORS

Education plays a critical role in promoting sustainable fashion. Today's problems and challenges are an opportunity for students to explore current systems, while driving positive change for the future. Some schools are working with fashion organizations and brands to investigate the impact of fast fashion. For instance, Traid, a UK charity working to reduce the impact of clothing waste, runs programs at schools on topics such as the product life cycle, upcycling and recycling, repairing and mending, good citizenship, and environmental stewardship. Interactive workshops and teamwork guide students toward a deeper understanding of current issues and provide an entry point for thinking critically.

Many colleges and universities weave the topic of sustainability into their curriculum as an expected practice for designers to incorporate into their own processes. Some approach sustainability from a systems perspective and ask students to design each part of the process not just the outcome. Organizations such as Fashion Revolution visit universities to raise awareness of the issues. Fashion Revolution also offers a selection of downloadable educational resources through its website and encourages participation in social media campaigns such as #WhoMadeMyClothes.

The Youth Fashion Summit is an educational platform and idea generator that "connects young industry talents from around the world giving them the opportunity to influence the decisions made today that impact the world of tomorrow, communicating the voice of the next generation."[135] The Youth Fashion Summit is closely linked to the Copenhagen Fashion Summit and the UN.

As they launch their careers, apparel designers and entrepreneurs have much to offer the industry, with their

Left: Youth Fashion Summit representatives present their demands for a sustainable fashion industry, 2019.

Right: Students work with industry leaders to draft resolutions to help solve the environmental challenges faced by the industry, 2019.

optimism and ambitions driving their creative ideas and innovations forward. However, many lack funding, or a road map (plan) to kick-start their businesses. Start-up accelerators (also known as seed accelerators) funded by brands and organizations can offer excellent opportunities for these entrepreneurs to acquire funding, mentorships, and the resources needed to advance their sustainable fashion careers. The Fashion for Good—Plug and Play Accelerator, based in Amsterdam, is an intensive program that works to find and scale innovative business models and technologies that have the greatest potential to help drive a shift toward a circular, sustainable fashion industry.

A sustainable fashion education can come from a variety of sources, including organizations, activists, and brands. The Fashion for Good Experience in Amsterdam is an interactive museum where visitors can learn how clothing is produced, discover sustainable products, and explore fashion innovations. Upon entry, visitors select an action bracelet to make sustainable commitments and earn badges to receive a personalized Good Fashion Action Plan. Participants can also design and customize a Cradle to Cradle certified T-shirt using their direct-to-consumer digital printer, or take photos in the Good GIF booth to share on social media.

INSPIRATIONAL FIGURES

Inspirational figures play an important role in leading others toward more circular solutions. In recognition of this, the World Economic Forum and the Forum of Global Leaders, in collaboration with Accenture Strategy, launched a circular economy awards program in 2014, called The Circulars. The award recognizes individuals and organizations in the public and private sectors who are making notable contributions to the circular economy.

INNOVATION

Innovative technologies and business models have the greatest potential to reshape the fashion industry for good. Moving toward a circular fashion economy means working collectively. Rethinking and redesigning fashion from the materials to the infrastructure needed to create a closed-loop system requires new platforms for innovation, technology, and knowledge sharing.

SUSTAINABLE MATERIALS

Materials are the core of any fashion producer's environmental footprint. Synthetic fibers comprise two-thirds of the

The Fashion for Good museum,
Amsterdam, aims to educate
visitors about sustainable fashion.

approximately 100 million tons of virgin fibers used in the global fiber market.[136] Polyester originates from crude oil, and tiny fragments known as microplastics have turned up in the ocean, harming aquatic life and polluting the waters.

Changing to a sustainable material mix can reduce the environmental footprint of a fashion producer significantly. For example, Global Fashion Agenda's CEO Agenda estimates that replacing conventional cotton with its organic alternative can save up to 90% of the fresh water and 62% of the energy used currently.[137]

DIGITAL TRACEABILITY

A major challenge facing the global supply chain is lack of transparency and traceability. Many consumers would like access to more information about a garment, such as the type of materials used to create it and whether it was ethically produced, before making a purchase. Simultaneously, producers want to promote their sustainable products and protect their merchandise from counterfeiting.

Blockchain technology, developed by transparency-tech platform and consultancy Provenance.org, aims for the status of materials to be traceable and transparent along the length of a product's supply chain. A collaboration with Martine Jarlgaard was launched in 2017.

Blockchain technology has the potential to revolutionize fashion's supply chain. By scanning a barcode with a mobile device, consumers gain access to a host of information about that particular product, enabling them to verify the material composition and sustainability or circularity of a garment. This technology also ensures the information communicated to consumers is safe, credible, and reliable.

> **Blockchain: *a digital database containing information (such as records of financial transactions) that can be simultaneously used and shared within a large decentralized, publicly accessible network.***
> Merriam-Webster Dictionary

However, at present there are very few established standards that define how the blockchain network should operate. This, along with a lack of technical awareness among businesses and consumers, are hurdles that must be overcome before this technology is more widely adopted by the industry.[138]

RECYCLING TECHNOLOGIES

Recycling plays a crucial role in a circular fashion economy by minimizing waste and preserving natural resources. Small-scale innovative recycling technologies are on the rise as they aim to keep clothes out of landfills by processing them back into a reusable resource. However, each year, almost 60 million tons of new (virgin) fibers are used to make clothing and yet, in contrast to the paper, aluminum, and steel industries, fashion has no large-scale recycling program for end of use textiles.[139]

One of the greatest circularity challenges at present is developing the recycling technology needed to convert large volumes of textile waste into higher value reusable resources, along with the ability to scale up globally while remaining economically viable.

However, some progress is being made. In 2019, for instance, the UK startup Worn Again Technologies opened a pilot research and development facility so they could continue developing their newly patented polymer recycling technology. The Cradle to Cradle Certified™ process can separate, decontaminate, and extract polymers and cellulose from non-reusable textiles to create new products, supporting a closed loop system.

Similarly, Novetex Textiles Ltd. launched The Billie System in 2019. This innovative system upcycles textile waste without the use of water and without producing chemical waste, and is able to process up to three tons of recycled fiber each day. This fiber can then be combined with virgin materials to create new garments.

Ultimately, if we begin by designing for circularity, using less impactful materials, promoting rental and repair models, and applying reverse supply chain intelligence, we can make space for recycling technology to eventually catch up, so that today's resources can be regenerated to become the resources of tomorrow.

CIRCULAR LEADER: EVA KRUSE

Global Fashion Agenda is a leadership forum dedicated to facilitating industry-wide collaboration on issues of sustainability. Founded by Eva Kruse as a thought-leader and advocacy organization, the not-for-profit company is on a mission to take bold and urgent action on the fashion industry's harmful and wasteful practices.

Since 2009, Global Fashion Agenda has held the renowned Copenhagen Fashion Summit, a business-focused event that brings together key stakeholders to discuss the ways in which they can make their industry more sustainable.

(globalfashionagenda.com)

THINK PIECE: How can individuals, businesses, and educators collaborate to create innovative fashion products and services for the future? How can these products and services respond to the current challenges the industry faces?

CASE STUDY #5: RENEW

EILEEN FISHER: THE CIRCULAR FASHION DESIGNER

American fashion designer Eileen Fisher started her namesake clothing brand in 1984 with just $350 USD (£285) and a desire to create simple, comfortable clothing that would help improve the lives of women. Today, Eileen Fisher is a 40 percent employee-owned, B-Corp certified company, and a leader in sustainability.

The company began its clothing recycling program, known as "Green Eileen," in 2009, when it started taking back the brand's unwanted clothing from its customers. Since then, the initiative, now known as the Eileen Fisher Renew program, has diverted approximately 1.2 million discarded Eileen Fisher garments from landfills so that they can be remade, reused, repaired, or resold. Clothes that are too damaged to be repaired are deconstructed to create entirely new garments under the brand's Resewn label, produced in the Eileen Fisher Tiny Factory in Irvington, New York.

As Creative Lead for Eileen Fisher's Renew program, designer Lilah Horwitz navigates a fine line between artist, designer, and systems thinker. She studied at the Parsons School of Design in New York, where she chose Integrated Design, a smaller emerging program where she was able to major in both Fashion Design and Sustainable Design. Working with pioneers in the slow fashion and design thinking movements, she learned to question the industry's systems and practices, and developed her own design code, which she then implemented by starting her own collection.

At Eileen Fisher, Horwitz designs three specialty Resewn collections a year, which sell on eileenfisher.com and in select stores. According to Horwitz, these collections represent "a radical departure from retail as we know it, focused on disrupting the industry by presenting limited edition designs made from nothing new."

Circular design differs from traditional fashion design in that new ideas don't stem from imagination or inspiration, but from the clothing and textiles at hand, which must be overseen through deconstruction to reconstruction until you have a beautiful new product. According to Horwitz, one of the biggest challenges to working with used/damaged clothing is bringing it to scale: "As a designer, I spend the bulk of my time sorting through garments and pulling out pieces of interest. The most time-consuming part of the process is deconstruction. Each piece must be considered in its final state before taking it apart so [we don't] cut through a seam that might be saved for the next design. Since the collections cannot be sewn in any normal method of production, my sewing partners and I have developed a new language of construction. I work closely with them and they are a big part of the design process."

Horwitz believes it is worth the time, because younger generations are increasingly mindful of circularity: "They are savvy with secondhand clothing and know how to recognize value. One-of-a-kind will be the next big focus."

The future of fashion, therefore, is in the hands of designers who see the complexities of end-of-use supply chain processes (collecting, sorting, cleaning, repairing, remaking, recycling) as opportunities to solve the problem of textile waste and close the loop.

DISCUSSION QUESTIONS

1. Describe the similarities and differences between a traditional fashion designer and circular fashion designer.
2. What are the challenges of using discarded or damaged clothing as a material source?
3. Why are Renew garments referred to as "one-of-a-kind" garments? What makes these garments different than traditional Eileen Fisher pieces?

Top: Reclaimed clothing, prototypes, and creative tools in the design workspace at Eileen Fisher.

Above: The best features of multiple garments are stitched together during reconstruction.

Right: Damaged clothing is transformed into unique, one-of-a-kind designs that preserve the value of the textiles.

GLOSSARY

Agrarian economy A rural economy that is centered around agricultural labor and commodities.

Bast fiber Long fibers collected from the stem of certain plants to use in textile manufacture, e.g. flax, hemp, and jute

Batik A dyeing technique, originating in Indonesia, in which a wax resist is applied to a whole cloth before the dye is applied.

Biodegradability A material's capacity to be broken down by living organisms and decay over time.

Biomimicry The practice of learning from, and replicating, elements of nature to solve human design problems.

Carbon footprint The total carbon dioxide emissions caused by the actions of an individual, a company, a country, etc.

Carding A textile process that involves separating individual fibers, using a series of dividing and redividing techniques, so that they lie parallel to one another. This also ensures that most of the impurities are removed.

Cellulose A fiber made from the plant carbohydrate cellulose, whether naturally occurring (such as cotton, linen, nettle, etc.) or manufactured (e.g. lycell, modal, viscose).

Closed-loop system A processing system in which materials are recycled so that they can be reused.

Corporate social responsibility A company's sense of responsibility toward the community and environment (both ecological and social) in which it operates.

Cradle to Cradle (C2C) A sustainable business strategy based on the regenerative cycles of nature, i.e. a plant or organism's waste enriches the soil, thereby providing nutrients for another lifeform to grow.

Dematerialization To reduce or eliminate the amount of materials used in the making of a product.

Dioxin A highly toxic and polluting compound released as a by-product of some manufacturing processes.

Felting The act of combining or compressing certain fibers or hairs, such as wool and fur, to make felt.

Filament A very fine, slender fiber.

Geo-tag An electronic tag that assigns geographical metadata to various media.

Heavy metal A group of metallic chemical elements, typified by a relatively high density and atomic weight, that are toxic, particularly to the environment.

Life Cycle Assessment An analysis technique that assesses the environmental impacts of the various stages of a product's life cycle, from the origins of its materials up until it is disposed of or recycled.

Lyocell A form of rayon, a synthetic fiber, made from wood pulp that is sourced from sustainable tree farms.

Mercerization A textile process in which a chemical treatment is applied to cellulose fiber, commonly cotton, to increase its luster and affinity for dyes.

Microfiber A synthetic fiber made from ultrafine yarn that commonly comprises polyester and nylon.

Microplastic Plastic pieces that measure less than five millimeters and that make their way into our waterways, polluting the environment.

Milling Any process or application used in the creation of fabric from raw materials, such as combing, spinning, dyeing, weaving, and finishing.

Natural capital The world's stock of natural assets, which comprise renewable resources, such as light and wind, and non-renewable resources, such as minerals.

Open-loop system A processing system in which materials are recycled into other products. (i.e. a plastic bottle is transformed into a fiber).

Peer-to-peer Online communities that enable people of various backgrounds and interests to connect, collaborate, share, borrow, rent, or shop with others in real-time.

Per- and Polyfluorinated Chemicals (PFCs) A group of man-made organic chemicals containing fluorine, which is used as a stain- and water-repellent surface treatment for textiles.

Petroleum A naturally occurring liquid found beneath the earth's surface which can be refined into fuel.

Polyester A synthetic material derived from petrochemicals.

Polyethylene terephthalate (PET): Thermoplastic polymer resin of the polyester family that is used in synthetic fibers.

Polymer A high molecular substance from which manufactured fibers are produced.

Post-consumer waste Material waste generated by the consumer after they have used a product.

Pre-consumer waste Material waste generated in the supply chain's manufacturing process before the product reaches the consumer.

Rayon A fiber or textile made form regenerated cellulose (*see* cellulose fiber).

Revenue stream A company or organization's source of income.

Sizing The process of applying a protective adhesive coating to the surface of a warp yarn to minimize yarn breakages during weaving.

Smart factory A highly digitized and automated manufacturing facility in which human intervention is minimal.

Solvent A substance, usually a liquid, in which another solid or substance can be dissolved.

Start-up accelerator A program, usually fixed term and undertaken alongside other companies, intended to help a fledgling business grow. An accelerator usually includes some form of initial investment, mentorship, and education.

Touchpoint A point of contact and/or interaction between a business and its customers.

Wicking A process, most commonly used for outdoor or technical apparel, in which textiles are engineered or treated to keep moisture away from the skin, so that wearers remain dry, ventilated, and comfortable.